Set up and Run a Successful

FARM SHOP

Ruth Weiss

Typeset by Judith Edgley
Design by Gillian Glen, Stansted
Printed by Biddles Ltd., Woodbridge Park, Guildford, Surrey.

British Library Cataloguing in Publication Data

Weiss, Ruth
    Set up and run a successful farm shop.
    1. Agricultural industries farms shops
    I. Title
    381.'41

    ISBN 0–906137–20–9

Photographs

Ruth Weiss	–	Pages 28, 30, 34 (top), 56, 59, 61, 69, 72, 79, 86, 92, 108 (top)
David Thear	–	Outside covers, pages 8, 34 (bottom), 78, 108 (bottom), 112, 114

If you would like details of other books published by Broad Leys Publishing Company, write or telephone to Broad Leys Publishing Company, Buriton House, Station Road, Newport, Saffron Walden, Essex, CB11 3PL, England. Telephone: (0799) 40922.

Contents

Acknowledgements

Sincere thanks to John Evans and Tony Hales (ADAS, Reading) for their help and encouragement; and to the family for their tolerance which made it possible to abandon all pretence at housekeeping while this was written.

Definition of a Farm Shop

Any self-respecting book starts with a definition of its subject; this one is somewhat tentative. A farm shop is a retail outlet:
* Situated on a farm
* Based wholly or partly on the sale of home-grown or home-produced goods
* Seen as an adjunct to the main business of farming.

This definition permits the inclusion of the 'pin-money enterprise' but excludes the vast supermarket/garden centre/camping centre complex which has overtaken its farming origins and is better classed in the realms of 'big business'.

In this publication the emphasis is on the small to medium-sized enterprise grappling with the problems of establishment and growth.

Abbreviations

ADAS	Agricultural Development and Advisory Service
ATB	Agricultural Training Board
CoSIRA	Council for Small Industries in Rural Areas—see RDC
DOE	Department of the Environment
EEC	European Economic Community
MAFF	Ministry of Agriculture, Fisheries and Food
NFU	National Farmers Union
PYO	Pick-Your-Own
RDC	Rural Development Commission (formerly CoSIRA)
VAT	Value Added Tax

Introduction

Diversification is in vogue. The farming press is full of examples of alternative farm enterprises. Capital grants for certain new enterprises, including farm shops, were introduced in January, 1988. It is tempting to jump on the band wagon. This book explores the possibilities and pitfalls of setting up a farm shop; especially the pitfalls.

Part 1 is divided into three chapters. Chapter 1 gives theoretical costings showing the effect of type of farm shop and scale of enterprise on profitability. Chapter 2 gives actual costings for our own 'part-success, part-failure' farm shop; it conveys particular warnings relating to bought-in produce. Chapter 3 outlines the steps involved in setting up a farm shop.

Part 2 of the book, an 'A to Z of farm shops' is intended to be used as a reference section. It includes a diverse mix of topics. Practical topics, based largely on our own experience, necessarily reflect our own preoccupation with fruit and vegetables. The somewhat patchy treatment of theoretical and statistical topics reflects a dearth of material relating specifically to farm shops.

Our search for information started in 1981 when we inherited an ailing farm shop on our new holding. We asked a lot of questions about farm shops but were unable to find many answers. Now, seven years on, we have some of the answers to some of the questions that we asked when we took over. We hope our gleanings will be of benefit to others.

Ruth Weiss

Effective display is half the fun and art of shopkeeping.

PART ONE

'The aim of all legitimate business is service, for profit, at a risk.' Benjamin C. Leeming.

Chapter One Costings

If you are thinking of setting up a farm shop you will need to make many decisions. The most basic are:

The three Ws	—	WHAT to sell
		WHOM to sell it to
		WHERE to sell it from
The three HOWs	—	HOW to get started
		HOW big you want to grow
		HOW to achieve this growth

The possibilities and pitfalls in setting up and developing a farm shop are best illustrated by looking at costings for different size and type of enterprise. Four groups of enterprise are considered:

A. Selling free range eggs. Example of an enterprise selling goods produced specifically for a retail outlet on the farm.

B. Selling top fruit. Example of a retailing activity added to an established farm enterprise.

C. Retailing bought-in produce.

D. Selling a mixture of home-grown, home-produced and bought-in goods.

A. Free range eggs – an addition to the farm economy.

If you keep five hens because you enjoy keeping five hens. because the children enjoy collecting the eggs, and because there are no eggs like your own—that's great. Forget the costings!

If you keep five hens this year with the intention of keeping 50 hens next year and 500 the year after, and you have visions of further expansion and farm shop sales, then you *must* keep accounts. Full accounts; Version 1 in Table 1 will not do! The figures in Version 1 may be strictly correct but they are totally misleading and it is all too easy, in a moment of mad optimism, to dream up:

5 hens	margin	£ 61.50
50 hens	margin	£ 615.00
500 hens	margin	£6150.00

Obviously, this example is absurd.

Table 1. Pin-money 'accounts' for five free range hens.

Version 1. DANGEROUS.

Sales (s) £

100 dozen eggs at 90p[1.]	*90.00*
5 boiling fowl	*2.50*
	92.50

Costs (c) £

5 pullets @ £3	*15.00*
5 sacks tail corn[2]	*15.00*
1 tin flea powder	*1.00*
	31.00

Margin for year (s−c)	*£61.50*

Version 2. Boring but REALISTIC.

Sales (s) £

Eggs at retail price[1.]	*90.00*
Eggs at packing station price	*none*
Boiling fowl	*2.50*
	92.50

Costs (c) £

5 pullets	*15.00*
Feed[2.]	*15.00*
Labour (production, sales)	*not accounted for*
Services (electricity etc.)	*not accounted for*
Office costs, advertising	*not accounted for*
Miscellaneous costs	*1.00*
Capital cost, repairs	*not accounted for*
	31.00

Margin for year (s−c)	*£61.50*

1. *Egg production taken at a pessimistic 240 per hen per year as compared with 260 according to Nix (1987) for average free range egg production. 90p/dozen taken as average retail price for free range eggs for Home Counties in 1986/87.*

2. *Feeding based on table scraps and tail corn.*

Version 2 of Table 1 is boring, but it is realistic in indicating some of the hidden inputs which may not apply (or can realistically be ignored) on the small scale but which become realities on scaling up. The effect of expanding to 50 hens is shown in Table 2. The margin for this size of flock is £400. Valuing your time at £2.50 an hour would allow you 26 minutes per day for tending the hens and selling the eggs. Does this make sense? The answer depends on your answer to the following:

* How much time does it actually take you to produce and retail eggs?
* How do you value your time? Are you mopping up 'spare' time that would otherwise be wasted or could your time be more profitably used in some other way?
* Do you enjoy having hens in the yard and customers at the door?
* Does your enterprise fit in with an overall development plan for farm and shop?

Table 2. Accounts for 50 free range hens.

Sales (s) £

1000 dozen eggs at retail price 90p[1]	900.00
Eggs at packing station price	none
Boiling fowl	25.00
	925.00

Costs (c) £

50 pullets	150.00
Feed[2]	350.00
Labour[3]	not accounted
Running costs[4]	25.00
Capital cost[5]	not accounted
	525.00

Margin for year (s−c)	£400.00

1. *See Note 1 of Table 1*
2. *Feed costs taken at £7 per hen per year (based on Nix 1987). The benefit of the 'food for free' table scraps and tail corn cannot be applied on this scale.*
3. *Assumes family labour only.*
4. *Running costs taken at 50p per hen per year (based on Nix 1987).*
5. *Capital costs not taken into account for this size of flock. It is assumed that buildings and equipment are available on the farm at opportunity cost.*

Clearly, 50 hens can give only a modest margin but such a venture can be very worthwhile for feeling your way into farm shop sales.

Farm shop scale

Would scaling up to 500 hens justify setting up a farm shop? Figures for a 500 bird enterprise are given in Table 3. For 500 birds the margin of £3900 has to cover labour and profit. Costing your own labour at farmworker rates means allowing £750 for labour (£1.50 per bird) for production. This leaves £3150 for retailing costs and profit. Whether this is worthwhile depends on the retailing outlet:

* The cost of setting up and running a farm shop will not be covered. You cannot run a farm shop for the sake of a 500 hen unit; £3150 a year will cover the labour for staffing a shop for only 24 hours per week.

* Selling through an existing farm shop makes sense as the overheads are then spread over a range of products. (£3150 for 10,000 dozen eggs sold per year gives a retailing margin of 31p per dozen eggs which compares well with the margin you would get by buying in free range eggs for resale.)

Backdoor sales of 10,000 dozen eggs a year from 500 hens means selling an average of 27 dozen eggs a day. If you are busy and resent the constant interruption of customers at the door, £3150 for producing and selling the eggs may seem a paltry reward. If, on the other hand, you enjoy the coming and goings of customers because you are stuck at home with the children, or if Granny is hungry for human contacts and a little enterprise of her own, then £3150 may prove to be a social and financial lifeline.

The figures for a 5000 hen unit look, on the face of it, much more promising. £31,500 is a substantial sum for

Table 3. Accounts for 500 and 5000 free range hens.

Sales (s) £	500 hens	5000 hens
Output, eggs per year	10,000 dozen	100,000 dozen
Sales at 90p per dozen[1]	9000	90,000
Costs (c) £		
Feed[2]	3500	35,000
Livestock depreciation[3]	850	8,500
Variable costs[4]	250	2,500
Housing & Equipment[5]	500	5,000
	5,100	51,000
Margin for year (s−c)	£3,900	£39,000

1. Assumes all eggs sold retail–very unlikely for the larger enterprise.
2. Assumes feed cost of £7 per hen per year.
3. Assumes £1.7 per hen per year.
4. Assumes 50p per hen per year.
5. Housing taken at £10 per hen per year, written off over about 10 years.

covering farm shop overheads BUT . . . 100,000 dozen eggs a year (an average of 275 dozen a day) is a mountain of eggs to sell and you would need well over a thousand customers a week to shift it. This is feasible only in an area with a very high population density and very low competition. If half the eggs have to be sold at lower prices–to retailers or to caterers or to packing stations–the sums look very different:

50,000 dozen eggs at 90p	£45,000
50,000 dozen eggs at 50p	£25,000
Total output	£70,000
Margin (£70,000–£51,000)	£19,000

N.B. Under new 1989 regulations *all* sales outlets of eggs no matter how small must be registered.

Summing up

* A pin money enterprise can be fun.
* A small unit,which makes use of family labour and existing buildings can be worthwhile. Similarly, selling eggs into an existing farm shop can be worthwhile.
* Expansion into a purpose built farm shop with employed labour is best avoided until you are certain that retail sales can be built up to a high enough level to justify the costs involved.

B. Retailing apples; extension of an existing farm venture.

Many farm shops have grown out of PYO ventures or developed from an existing mainstay of the farm. If you grow apples as a main farm activity, if you grade and pack the fruit in a pleasant packing shed operating five days a week, and if the shed is readily accessible from a road with much passing traffic, you are ideally placed to venture into retailing. Simply put up a sign at the roadside, ensure that you have parking space near the shed, set up an attractive display of fruit in a corner of the shed (your only major outlay will be on scales, lighting, and packaging) and wait for the action. Customers will enjoy the working atmosphere. Staff will enjoy the occasional switch to sales and public relations work. Profitability depends on the extra value gained by selling the fruit retail rather than wholesale.

Retailing from a packing shed.

Table 4 shows costings for retail sales of apples from an established fruit farm. The examples assume an average wholesale price of 16p per lb and an average retail price of 26p, giving a margin of 10p per lb to cover costs and profit. Stage 1 of Table 4, for a small-scale outlet based in the packing shed, shows that sales of 150 lb apples per week are needed to cover the token cost ascribed to labour.

Increasing sales would justify weekend opening; low-cost student help at weekends has been included in Stage 2. It is clear that a gradual increase in sales can be accommodated without much further expense until such time as the sales begin to interfere with the smooth operation of the packing shed. At this point a deliberate decision has to be

Table 4. Sales of fruit needed to reach break-even point.

All stages assume: | Average wholesale price | 16p/lb
Average retail price | 26p/lb
Margin | 10p/lb

Stage 1. Small-scale retailing from packing shed during normal working hours only.

Weekly costs: | Labour[1] | £15
Other costs[2] | nil
_____
£15

Sales to break even : 150 lb fruit/week (retail sales value £39)

Stage 2. Sales increasing. Retailing from packing shed during normal working hours. Also open at weekends.

Weekly costs: | Labour, as above | £15
Weekend labour (£2/hour) | £32
Packaging | £ 2
Equipment costs | £ 2
Office/Advertising | £ 2
_____
£53

Sales to break even : 530 lb fruit/week (retail sales £138)

Stage 3. Sales from farm shop. (Packing shed facilities outgrown)

Weekly costs: | Labour[3] & running costs[4] | £225
Capital charge[5] | £40
_____
£265

Sales to break even: 2650 lb/week (retail sales value £689)

Notes:
1. One hour per day (£3) as portion of packing shed labour.
2. Other costs ignored at this stage.
3. 50 hours at £2.50.
4. Taken at 80% of labour costs.
5. Averaged out as an annual charge.

made either to stop advertising and consolidate at the low-input stage or to take the leap into a farm shop venture.

Retailing from a farm shop.

A leap to a separate farm shop is likely to be expensive, necessitating separate premises and separate staffing. Stage 3 of Table 4 shows that such a move would be warranted only for greatly increased sales. (Retail sales of about £700 per week are needed to cover basic shop expenses; further sales are needed to cover a return for family labour, management time and profit.)

Summing up

Retailing of produce grown as a mainstay of the farm gives an ideal low-risk entry into farm gate sales. The move to a farm shop is best delayed until it is certain that there will be enough customers to warrant the capital input involved.

C. Retailing bought-in goods

Success or failure in retailing bought-in goods depends largely on the scale of the operation. Examples are given below of the tiny, small and medium scale enterprise.

Example one: Strawberries and cream

Buying-in on a tiny scale e.g. cream to go with home-grown strawberries, is an extra service appreciated by customers. It makes economic sense, as the only costs involved are refrigeration and occasional wastage. Other costs such as labour can be covered by the strawberry enterprise. The sale of 100 half-pint cartons of double Jersey cream gives a sales margin over the cost of the cream of £27 (at 1988 prices). A word of warning: do not get greedy. Success depends on staying small and thus escaping heavy overhead costs.

Buying-in is usually justified if farm gate sales of home produce (e.g. eggs) are already established and under-utilised labour and premises are available. In such cases the addition of a few lines of fresh bought-in produce can help to draw in additional customers at little extra cost.

Example two: The Trap (see Table 5)

This example of a shop selling fruit, vegetables and whole-foods to the value of £1000 per week is given as a warning. It shows what happens when a shop is large enough to attract all the costs and commitments of a retail outlet but not large enough to benefit from economy of scale. Much money changes hands but very little seems to stick. It is a financial merry-go-round. It is also a trap because the owner is so busy rolling up his sleeves and dodging between the buying, selling, management and bookwork that he may fail to notice what is happening.

The happenings are quite simple. The business is lumbered with considerable capital and running costs but lacks the turnover to cover these and to leave a sensible return for management and profit. A reward of £1700 for a year's operation may be acceptable in the early stages of development but a business that sticks there will leave the owner without time to think, without money for further investment and without hope of future profit.

Example three: A viable business

The 'Viable' example (see Table 5) gives costings for a shop with sales of £2000 per week. This is about the level of sales of the average High Street greengrocer in 1987. (It is a sobering thought that the High Street greengrocer is a rapidly declining species, so beware of complacency even at this level of sales.) The figures have been extrapolated from the Trap to show the effect of scaling-up. Some costs are not affected by scaling-up; others are taken as doubled. The annual sales of £104,000 leave a margin of £8,275 to cover family labour, management and profit.

Summing up

The aim of these examples is to illustrate the effect of economy of scale in retailing bought-in goods. It is all too easy to be trapped into a business which 'feels' as if it is flourishing but is structurally too small.

Table 5. Costings for bought-in produce.

Sales (s)	Example two THE TRAP[1] £/year £52,000	Ex.[2] x 2.0	Example three VIABLE £/year £104,000
Costs			
Wages[3]	£ 5,250	x 2.0	£ 10,500
Bank charges	£ 200	x 1.5	£ 300
Accountancy	£ 300	x 1.5	£ 450
Telephone/Office	£ 350	x 1.5	£ 525
Advertising	£ 900	x 1.5	£ 1,350
Heat/light/water	£ 450	x 1.5	£ 675
Transport	£ 700	x 1.25	£ 875
Insurance	£ 200	x 1.25	£ 250
Rates	£ 600	same	£ 600
Repairs/renewals	£ 600	x 1.25	£ 750
Packaging	£ 500	x 2.0	£ 1,000
Miscellaneous	£ 300	x 1.5	£ 450
Total running costs(r)	£10,350		£ 17,725
Annual charge[4] (c)	£ 2,000		£ 2,000
Purchases (p)	£38,000		£ 76,000
Trading margin s − (p + r)	£ 3,650		£ 10,275
Profit margin s − (p + r + c)	£ 1,650		£ 8,275
Profit margin (as % of sales)	3.2%		8.0%

Notes:

1. Based on data for sales of fruit, vegetables and wholefoods at Mortimer Hill Farm Shop, 1981–86.

2. By extrapolation from Example two. Some expenses e.g. rates, stay the same; others e.g. transport, increase only slightly; others e.g. wages, increase pro rata.

3. Wages based on adult help during the week and youngsters at the weekend i.e:
    28 hours at £2.75/hour   = £ 77/week
    12 hours at £2.00/hour   = £ 24/week
    Total   = £101/week
    This excludes own and family labour.

4. Annual charge—see section on 'Capital inputs'. The annual charge has been spread equally over the years but is actually heavier in the first years of operation.

D. Mixed sales. The farm shop scene.

'All the business of war, and indeed all the business of life, is to endeavour to find out what you don't know by what you do; that's what I call "guessing what was at the other side of the hill".' Arthur Wellesley, Duke of Wellington, 1885.

The foregoing examples assumed that sales were based on one type of product (eggs produced specially for retailing from the farm, apples already grown on the farm) or bought -in goods. In reality a farm shop is likely to be more complex and involve a mix of activities so that guessing what might be on 'the other side of the hill' is even more difficult. The following example assumes a combination of home-grown and bought produce. It can give only an imprecise picture of costings but is, nevertheless, useful for learning what can reasonably be estimated and what must be risked.

The example is based on a farm which already has a modest top fruit enterprise with sales geared to the whole-sale market; a small packing shed operates from September to March (weekdays only). There is sufficient space in the packing shed for small-scale retail sales. Alternatively, an old stable building could be converted into a farm shop. Buildings have adequate access and parking space. The farmer's wife keeps 25 free range hens and would be happy to expand this—extra buildings are available for housing up to 250 hens. A relative on a nearby farm grows potatoes, cabbages, onions and sweetcorn which could be bought-in to mutual advantage. Mother-in-law does a good line in herb jellies (using blemished apples and home-grown herbs) which she would like to market.

Has this got the makings of a farm shop? How do you start to work things out? First, sort out the priorities—in this case the home-grown fruit gives the basis for the shop sales; fruit is available for eight months of the year and retail sales involve neither risk nor waste. Size up the other possibilities. Hens around the yard and free range eggs in the shop are an asset. Projections for sale of eggs can be linked to fruit sales—maybe one in three customers would buy eggs i.e. one dozen eggs sold per three customers buying fruit? The sale of fresh local vegetables would be an extra draw provided that transport could be easily fitted into the farm routine and that sales space was available. Work on the assumption of every other customer buying one pounds worth of goods i.e. 50p per customer. Herb jellies? They could become a great attraction but it is difficult to forecast how quickly sales would build up and how well the idea would scale-up. It seems safest to encourage this enterprise but to exclude it from the financial projections at this stage.

The weakest link in making financial projections is predicting the number of customers you are likely to attract. You can count traffic flow, study population densities in the surrounding area, look at other farm shops, count people in and out of local supermarkets and High Street shops, read academic reports on marketing and seek advice. All these are worthwhile and will help your guess to be more informed. It will remain a guess.

The classic way to dodge this problem is to work on the break even system. Tot up all costs and margins, calculate how many customers are needed to cover basic costs. The question then changes from 'How many customers can we attract?' to 'Can we attract x customers a day?' Putting it this way makes the question more specific and easier to come to grips with, as it requires only a yes/no answer.

Farm shop—break even calculation

1. Expenditure per customer:

(a) *Assume that fruit is the major sales item. Assume average of 7.5 lb fruit per customer, price 26p/lb.*
Average expenditure on fruit £1.95.

(b) *Assume one in three customers buys a dozen eggs.*
Average expenditure on eggs £0.30.

(c) *Assume half the customers spend £1.00 on vegetables.*
Average expenditure on vegetables £0.50.
Average total expenditure/customer £2.75.

2. Margins:

(a) *Apples. Wholesale price 16p, retail price 26p. (no wastage, no transport as apples already on the farm)*
Margin on sales $\frac{10}{26} \times 100 = 36\%$

(b) *For eggs and vegetables assume a margin on sales of 28%.*

3.   Margin per customer:

38% on fruit sales, £1.95	*=74p*
28% on egg & vegetables sales, 80p	*=22p*
Margin on sale per customer	*96p*

4.   Number of customers needed to cover expenses:

	Sales from packing shed	Sales from farm shop
Cost of running retail outlet (£/week)	£53[1]	£265[2]
Customers/week to break even	55	276

Notes: 1. Table 4, stage 2   2. Table 4, stage 3

This example, for all its assumptions, shows that starting a shop as an adjunct to an existing enterprise and adding in other products for sale can give you: a low-risk start; valuable experience; and useful figures for subsequent planning.

   The move from a corner of the packing shed to separate farm shop premises with separate staffing involves a leap from 55 to 280 customers per week simply to cover costs. It is wise to avoid such a leap until you are certain that customer numbers will warrant it.

Summary

The aim of the costings in this chapter is to show how type of enterprise and size of enterprise affect profitability. Making use of products on the farm and of existing staff and facilities gives an ideal low-cost low-risk opportunity to 'test the water'. Bought-in produce involves more work, more risk and modest margins but can add variety, and support the home produce.

Size of enterprise is crucial (see 'Scale of operation'). A tiny enterprise can be very profitable. A well established farm shop with a regular throughput of several hundred customers a week can contribute a steady income to the farm. Between the two lies a danger zone where size of business is too large to benefit from 'opportunity-use' of resources and too small to benefit from economies of scale. You may need to go through this zone whilst building up the shop: to stick there spells disaster.

Chapter Two Mortimer Hill Farm – a case history

'A business that makes nothing but money is a poor kind of business.' Henry Ford, 1919.

In 1981 we took down the fences, ploughed up the grassland and started planting up eight acres of soft fruit. We set up our future PYO unit with confidence based on a lifetime in farming, six years experience in PYO, a good site within easy reach of an expanding population in Berkshire's Silicon Valley and no close competitors. We had detailed cropping plans and detailed financial projections thanks to ADAS technical and management advice. Our targets were modest; our cash-flow projections caused no sleepless nights.

By contrast, our venture into the farm shop was a leap in the dark. We did not plan to set up a shop—we were confronted with it when we took over the holding. We had no experience of retailing, we knew of no one who could guide us and ADAS advice was restricted to lively interest tempered by professional caution.

Our reasons for taking on the farm shop were:

* To establish a base for future sales of our own crops.
* To provide a secondary income to mitigate the effect of a possible PYO disaster season, and to even out the seasonality of income.
* The shop was there, it was well sited, potentially attractive, and had a small core of customers. It was a challenge.

The start; 1981 to 1982

We took over the farm shop in the depth of winter in 1981. The weather and the shop were horribly cold. The shop was not particularly welcoming and stocked a strange mix of goods. It would be eighteen months before our own crops started to come in.

During the first two years we felt our way slowly into retailing. Our first change was to reduce the mix of products; we decided to concentrate on fruit and vegetables in order to set the scene for our own future produce. We opted for the quality market, and aimed at a full range of fruit and vegetables, highlighting a wide selection of locally grown produce. We learned a lot and made a point of passing on to our customers as much information as possible about the goods we stocked; this educational role and insistence on quality helped to establish our image.

During this initial period we developed our links with local growers and found our way around the wholesale market; we reduced to a minimum our dependance on secondary wholesalers.

We reduced shop opening from seven days a week to only four. At the same time we phased out the existing staff and took on the work ourselves. Our input of time (for buying, selling and management) seemed enormous in relation to our turnover but we ascribed this to learning costs. Wastage too was high in relation to turnover (minimum pack size of watercress, red peppers and aubergines was often more than we could sell).

The first year's trading, with a turnover of only £25,000 and high labour costs (due to 'inherited' staff) resulted in a loss. In the second year turnover increased by more than 20% and all running costs were covered. We improved the heating, lighting and layout inside the shop; and the landscaping and leisure facilities around it. Things began to feel right by the time our own produce started coming in.

Development phase ; 1983–1986

From 1983 to 1986 the shop continued to make steady progress with an average increase in turnover of 22% per year (see Figure 1). The increase was particularly marked during the summer, rising more or less in proportion to the rising PYO sales. The PYO and farm shop enterprises dovetailed and appeared to be mutually beneficial.

The winter months continued to be problematic. In an attempt to attract more winter trade and to increase expenditure per customer we widened the range of goods, adding wholefoods, organically-grown foods, home-made baked goods and preserves. The wholefoods were a success, we got into the right market at the right time and they fitted in well with our greengroceries. The organic venture was a failure: we certainly had the demand—customers were prepared to travel a long way to get good produce and were prepared to pay a premium for it. Unfortunately we could not obtain a continuous supply of first class produce and we were unwilling to compromise on quality. Sales of home-made goods and of our own frozen fruit flourished.

As our product range increased, so the complexity of our buying, selling and management increased. We were handling upwards of 70 lines of fruit and vegetables and 200 lines of wholefoods at any one time, in addition to our own produce. We added part-time staff to help in the shop. We continued to operate on a four day a week basis during the winter, changing to daily opening during the fruit season.

Turnover increased from under £50,000 in 1984 to over £70,000 in 1986 and trading margin reached £6000 in 1986. This had to cover the labour and management input of full-time wife with part-time help from husband and family. We were still on unfirm ground; if one of us became ill and we needed to employ full-time management and labour to replace the family input, the shop operation would be a liability rather than an asset. We reckoned we needed a further growth of 15% per year for another two or three years in order to feel secure.

1987

The year 1987 proved to be the year of reckoning. We did not achieve further growth; sales of bought-in goods remained close to the 1986 level (see Figure 1). In summer, the shop sales continued to peak together with the peak PYO sales (see Figures 2 and 3). Both PYO and shop turnover were almost the same in 1987 as in 1986. (In previous years PYO was still increasing as the canes and bushes came into maturity but yields had now stabilized.) As we did not anticipate further dramatic increases in yields of our own produce and as sales of bought-in produce appeared to follow the PYO sales, it seemed unlikely that summer sales of bought-in produce would increase.

Winter sales also appeared to have levelled off; the number of local customers is inherently limited by the size of the local population. We know that we can attract customers from further afield in the summer, by virtue of our own fresh produce and the attraction of 'a run out to the country'; in winter we have no advantages over supermarkets.

Decisions

We made the following decisions:

* To close the shop at the end of the 1987 picking season and to remain closed over the winter.

* To re-open with the first crops of the year (rhubarb and asparagus) in May. We shall be open, initially, at weekends only, changing to daily opening for the main soft fruit season.

* To concentrate all our efforts on home-grown and home-made produce. We shall continue to extend the range of crops grown, but only in so far as this fits in with existing cultural techniques and expertise, aiming, for instance, at extending the season of the crops that we already grow. We shall continue to increase our range of home-made goods and, above all, to promote the leisure facilities.

* To discontinue selling bought-in produce except for the obvious adjuncts to the soft fruit, such as cream and jam pot covers.

Why did it take us so many years to reach this decision? The continued growth in sales to 1986 lulled us into unjustified optimism. We failed to anticipate that summer sales of bought-in produce would level off in line with the maturation of the PYO unit. We also failed to react to the relatively slow rate of growth in winter trade, failing to appreciate that, however attractive the shop, it did not lure enough customers to the farm during the winter (see Figure 4).

Evaluation

The PYO is now firmly established and the shop has achieved our aim of helping to set the scene for the sale of our own produce.

We have sunk much time and effort into the shop but this has not been wasted; we have gained a great deal of experience and retain the basic shop framework for the future. Our only regret at closing the shop over the winter is in relation to the small but faithful core clientele who braved the drive to the farm in all winds and weathers.

Summing up

On the negative side we have learned that we cannot compete with the supermarkets as regards one-stop shopping, proximity to customers and economy of scale, especially in winter. On the positive side, we are confident that in summer no supermarket can compete with our home-grown fruit or our facilities for a family outing. The shop has served us well in setting the stage for our own produce; we are now happy to abandon the bought-in goods and to close in the winter. We are confident that doing less and doing it well is our best policy.

Figure 1. Annual Turnover* 1981–87 Mortimer Hill Farm Shop

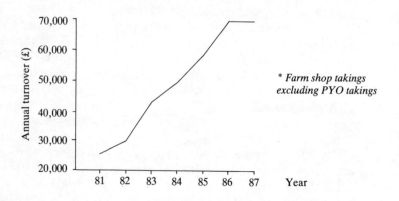

* Farm shop takings excluding PYO takings

Figure 2. Seasonality of sales*, Mortimer Hill Farm Shop, 1986–87

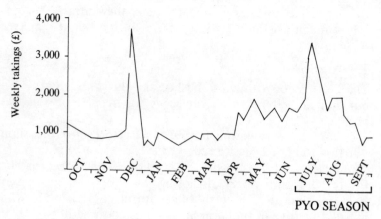

*Farm shop takings excluding PYO takings

Figure 3. Monthly sales* as % of annual sales Mortimer Hill 1986—87

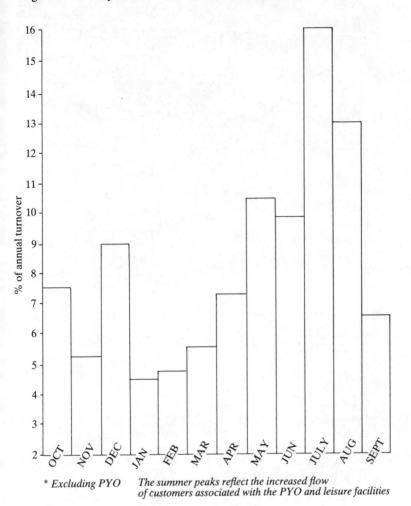

* Excluding PYO   *The summer peaks reflect the increased flow of customers associated with the PYO and leisure facilities*

Figure 4. Summer : Winter sales as % of total sales*
Mortimer Hill Farm Shop 1986—87

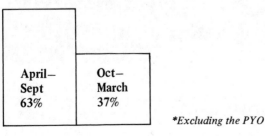

April—
Sept
63%

Oct—
March
37%

Excluding the PYO

Low risk enterprises. A simple lean-to near the farmhouse door (top) or a small retail section at the end of a fruit packing shed (bottom) make good use of available labour.

Chapter Three Starting up

'Direct selling requires a large scale increase in marketing responsibility, and although farmshops, self-pick crops and farmer-run shops or garden centres may all seem attractive propositions, any inclusion of direct sales into the farm business should be planned with great deliberation. Basically the farmer should "look before he leaps" in order to avoid a financially perilous fall.' Barker, 1981.

The vision
Grab a pen and paper! Write down any random thoughts about the farm shop you envisage, especially size, image and financial expectations.

Initial assessment
Stop dreaming and sum up the realities:

*   List the main factors in setting up shop:
  potential goods
  potential customers
  resources such as location, buildings, finance, labour, knowledge, enthusiasm
*   List your strengths and your weaknesses
*   Read Chapter 1 on Costings and the section on Retail statistics
*   Try some back-of-envelope figures to work out how many customers you would need to cover costs and how many to achieve your financial expectations (use the sections on Capital inputs, Running costs, Cash flow and Mark-up and margins to help you with the 'guesstimates').

Initial decision making
If your ideas seem feasible carry on below. If not amend them or scrap them.

Feasibility studies
Unless you have decided to set up on such a small scale that you run virtually no risk, get help at this stage (see Appendix 2 on sources of advice). It is far better to pay for financial and management help now than to pay for mistakes later.

A growing commitment. These separate farm shops, whether near the farm buildings (top) or near the farmhouse (bottom) involve capital investment and regular staffing.

* Get the farm shop idea into perspective in relation to the entire farm business—give thought particularly to the demands on labour and management at peak seasons.
* Firm up on trading projections. To do this you will have to check the initial assessments you made, with brave projections of customer numbers, average expenditure per customer, mark-up on the type of goods you plan to sell and estimates of running costs.
* Use the trading projections and estimates of capital inputs to prepare cash flow projections. These will be needed for your own decision making, for adjusting your targets, and for supporting bank loan or grant applications (see Borrowing and Diversification Grants).
* Technical advice may be needed to plan crop production or produce manufacture.
* It is sensible to approach the local authorities at this stage for a preliminary discussion of your project and for guidance as to the likelihood of obtaining planning consent.
* If you are a tenant you should talk to your landlord about your plans.
* Make sure you have the approval and the backing of your family.

Final decision making

If your ideas still make sense carry on below. If not amend them or scrap them.

Action. Phase 1

* Put your bank manager and accountant in the picture if you have not already done so.
* Finalise your plans for buildings and apply for planning permission as required.
* Apply for other permission as required, depending on the produce to be sold. Health Authority approval is particularly important if you are going to deal in dairy products, meat or cooked foods.
* Apply for diversification grant if applicable.
* Finalise your production plans for crops or whatever produce you intend to sell.

Action. Phase 2

* Once you have the necessary approvals from the authorities you can go ahead with building, and with work on access and parking.
* You can get started on growing or production.
* While these major activities are under way see to:
  Purchase of equipment for the shop (see Equipment).
  Shop layout and furnishings (see Layout).
  Staffing decisions (see Staffing).
  Decisions about opening times (see Opening times).
  Advertising policy (see Advertising, Signposting and Public relations).
  Setting up a system of accounting and record keeping (see Accounts, Money and Records).
  Insurance (see Insurance).

The opening

Blow your own trumpet and get news of your opening into the press. Make it an Occasion and keep the press well informed.

Monitoring progress

Keep full records and make a point of keeping your fingers on the pulse of the business by constant monitoring of results and referring back to compare with your targets. Do not expect fast growth—the best advertisement is by word of mouth; shop trade builds up steadily rather than dramatically. However, do not simply shrug off disappointing results—face them, analyse them, and try to rectify them.

PART TWO
An A–Z
of Farm Shops

Traffic requires careful routing and signposting (top). Convenient and clearly signed parking attracts customers (bottom).

Access and parking

'Consult your planners first—not last—to help with accident-free access and car park.' Hew Watt, 1988.

Beware of underestimating the importance of access and parking. A healthy farm shop generates a healthy flow of traffic. Healthy from the farmer's viewpoint. Not necessarily from the viewpoint of the local residents, local planning authority, highway authority, the police and the Department of the Environment.

In 1984 a Yorkshire farmer with a small herd of Channel Island cows embarked on an exemplary scheme of diversification, turning 90,000 litres of milk a year into high quality ice cream (Farmers Weekly, 1988). He was so successful that within four years his fame had spread over hill and dale; customers flocked to the farm. Two-thirds of his output was retailed direct from the farm at Wescoe Hill near the small village of Weeton; a shining light according to the Gospel of Diversification as expounded by the Ministry of Agriculture.

The Department of the Environment thought otherwise. The venture had been set up with due consent of the planning authorities but its success brought traffic and traffic brought complaints. Parked cars, vehicle movement and the noise of happy ice cream lickers were deemed to disturb the tranquility of the countryside. Harrogate County Council brought an enforcement notice ordering cessation of retail sales from the farm. The farmer appealed. The Department of the Environment rejected the appeal, ordering the farmer to confine his activities to wholesale trading—for which he was not geared.

Such cases highlight the need for co-operation between the Ministry of Agriculture and the Department of the Environment. Pressure for a unified planning system is increasing but as yet there is little action. For the moment, therefore, it is prudent to bear these problems in mind.

Access: Cars must be able to reach your farm, to enter and to leave it without causing congestion on approach routes and without endangering the flow of passing traffic. If in doubt, ask your local policeman or highway authority for advice.

Traffic flow: It is impossible to make an accurate prediction of traffic flow to a farm shop. Nevertheless rough calculations can give some indication of what to expect. You will need to make brave assumptions: the example below relates to a farm shop open five days a week, with peak sales at summer weekends:

* Assume annual turnover of £100,000 with daily takings averaging about £400.
* Assume average customer expenditure of £2.00, thus average number of customers per day is 200.
* Assume two customers per car, thus average number of cars per day is 100. (Average number of cars per hour is 14.)
* Assume 50% of daily sales occur during three peak hours of the day, thus number of cars during peak times is 50 ÷ 3 i.e. about 17 per hour.
* Assume Saturday trade is double the average, thus number of cars during peak hours on Saturdays is 17 x 2 = 34.
* Assume summer trading is double the average for the year, thus the number of cars at peak hours on fine summer Saturdays is 34 x 2 = 68 per hour.

This rough calculation suggests that a modest average of 14 cars per hour might, albeit only occasionally, rise to an average of more than a car a minute entering and leaving your premises. Would this be feasible? And safe? Again, if in doubt, consult your local policeman or highway authority.

Parking: Similar calculations indicate the scale of parking requirements. In the example above, for an average flow of 14 cars per hour, and an average stay of 20 minutes, parking would be needed for five cars at a time. This would rise to six during the peak hours of an average day. Doubling the requirements for weekends and again for fine summer days suggests that parking for 24 cars would be required. The calculation is based on farm shop only. The addition of leisure facilities or PYO increases the duration of stay, with corresponding increase in parking needs; fortunately such activities occur mostly in fine weather when grass parking is adequate.

Accounts

Accounts for a farm shop enterprise must be separable from the farm accounts. This can be achieved by keeping a separate bank account for the shop, with separate sets of ledgers. The advantage of keeping totally separate accounts is that stubs and statements for each account indicate at any time exactly where each business stands. Alternatively, all farm enterprises can share bank account and ledger—but with separate analysis columns for farm and farm shop transactions. This obviates cheque book muddles, facilitates VAT calculations and makes it easy to deal with joint farm-plus-shop expenses such as electricity and water. Success depends on remembering to note 'farm' or 'shop' or 'joint expense' on each invoice at the time of payment. There is no right or wrong system. Choose whichever seems to suit you. If in doubt consult your accountant.

Adding value to farm produce

Adding value means packaging or processing produce into goods of higher value: milk into cheese, fruit into fruit juice, root vegetables into a 'soup pack', timber into furniture. It is easy on a small scale using existing farm or kitchen facilities and this often knits in well with a small farm shop.

Scaling-up requires considerable capital inputs as well as technical and marketing expertise. Nevertheless there is a demand for speciality goods and advice is becoming available thanks to the NFU Marketing Division, RDC (CoSIRA), local Enterprise Agencies and local marketing organisations (see Appendix 2). To get a feel of what others are doing browse through the *British Country Foods Directory* (see Appendix 1).

Is adding value for you? Much depends on aims, available raw material and customer demand.

Aims: Adding value has several potential aims and benefits:
* To gain a higher price for your produce.
* To add interesting produce to your shop and so attract more customers.
* To extend the season or to fill the gaps when you are short of fresh home-grown produce.
* To get your shop known for specialities that will draw customers down YOUR drive to YOUR farm shop for YOUR special produce.

Available raw material: Start with produce already on the farm e.g. turning wheat into home-milled flour or using bedding plants to make up hanging baskets. Processing is particularly useful for converting high quality but low value goods, such as small Cox apples, into a high value product such as apple juice; this is the basis of the Copella success story. Another success story comes from a small Devon farmer who found that the meat from her traditional breeds of pig fetched below-average market prices yet resulted in above-average bacon quality. Friends persuaded her to start processing meat products and this has led, via an NFU Marketing Award, to a highly successful marketing venture (Petch, 1986).

Surplus products can be put to good use. Bedding plants left over in late spring can be planted in tubs and window boxes for sale, flowering, in the summer. Surplus soft fruit can be picked into transparent containers and frozen for sale during the winter. Surplus tomatoes can be turned into chutneys or sauces. Damaged produce can be utilised. The possibilities are as long as your imagination. Be careful though to do your costings carefully. Adding value inevitably involves work and/or materials; make sure that your added costs are not greater than the added value.

Customer demand: *'You can't sell it unless you know what they want. So find out!'* advises Tony de Angelou, Editor of 'The Grocer'. The demand for fresh strawberries at Wimbledon time is perennial. The demand for other products is liable to change. Good marketing starts with an awareness of change. The born entrepreneur is skilled at sensing changing market demands. Various pointers can help: The National Food Survey statistics show broad areas of change; the national press and specialist trade journals also offer clues on trends in health and eating; TV cookery programmes reflect changing interests in food. Some trends in eating habits, and their possible implications for adding-value to farm shop enterprises are outlined below.

Flour and baked goods: The total household food consumption of biscuits, cakes and other cereal products remained fairly static from 1975–1985 after a steep decline in the previous decade. Since 1965, flour consumption has decreased by one-third, largely reflecting a decline in home baking. Consumption of bread fell between 1965 and 1980 but since then the total bread consumption has been fairly static; the interesting change is that while white bread sales have continued to decline, sales of wholemeal bread have risen markedly (see Figure 5). This information is useful if you are thinking of milling your own flour or selling home-baked bread. Put the emphasis on wholemeal and speciality flours; maybe a mixed loaf full of different grains and seeds, herb loaves, onion bread or cheese rolls? Consider baking them in a flower-pot for a special old-fashioned and rural effect. Use imagination, research and experiment-ation to find something you enjoy making, and which will give your shop a unique product.

Figure 5. Consumption of bread 1965–85

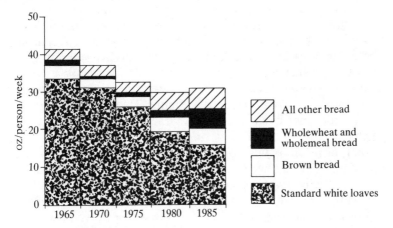

Source: National Food Survey

   The decline of home baking suggests other opportun-ities for the farm shop. Traditional baked goods such as fruit cake, gingerbread, shortbread and flapjacks 'like Granny used to make them' are appropriate to the farm shop scene and can become best sellers. Consider using wholemeal flour to bring traditional recipes into line with current trends in eating.

Fruit juices: The consumption of fruit juices in the UK has increased dramatically from under 1 oz per head per week in 1965 to about 5 oz in 1985 (see Figure 6). This is still well below average consumption in the USA and continued market growth is predicted.

Figure 6. Consumption of fruit juices 1965—85

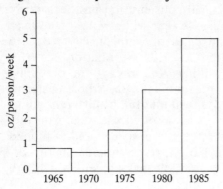

Source: National Food Survey

Supermarkets, grocers, greengrocers and dairies are in on the market, so does this leave scope for the farm shop? A grower with a farm shop might consider selling 'the real thing' as opposed to canned, cartoned and pasteurised juices. Freshly-pressed fruit and vegetable juices cannot be cheap but do fit the farm shop image. Give small tasters to get sales started.

Frozen convenience foods: Frozen convenience foods are another growth area (see Figure 7). This is not good news for the fresh produce market but if you cannot fight it then consider getting in on the act. Emulate a small farm shop which does a marvellous line in summer puddings from the freezer (it is one of the few dishes that actually *improves* on freezing). What could be more evocative of Granny-style cooking than this most English of desserts bursting with fruit and the flavour of summer?

Figure 7. Consumption of frozen convenience foods 1965—85

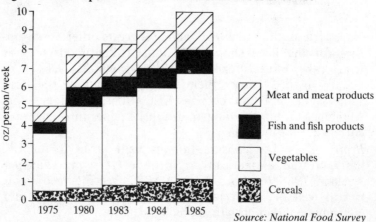

Source: National Food Survey

40

Preserves: The trend towards numerous quick meals and savoury snacks rather than three square meals a day gives increasing opportunity for accompanying chutneys, herb jellies and savoury sauces. Jams are a declining market (hit by the demise of afternoon tea) though there is still a demand for quality produce; also perhaps for low sugar versions?

Conclusion: No two farm shops are alike—that is what makes them a welcome antidote to the look-alike supermarkets and their taste-alike produce. Standardisation has many virtues but an excess is boring; this creates a useful niche for the small, the enterprising and the different. Customers will come to your shop, and keep on coming if you can give them goods or services that they cannot get elsewhere. Adding value to farm produce makes good sense if you can find suitable lines for your shop and if you can manage an appropriate scale of operation. The illustrations in this chapter are intended only to indicate the type of enterprise you might consider. The best ideas are the ones that no one has yet thought of.

Advertising

'Doing business without advertising is like winking at a girl in the dark. You know what you're doing, but no one else does.' Robert Penn Warren.

With a pin-money scale enterprise there is little need for advertising. A sign on the roadside (see under Signposting) and adverts in the local post office and parish magazine may well suffice. The best advertising is by word of mouth. Get out and chat at local meetings, at the school playground and at the pub. Initially your friends and neighbours will support you out of curiosity and loyalty. If there is a demand for your products, and if your shop is good they will carry on coming.

You need to think' carefully about the type of customers you hope to attract, where such customers live, and what form of advertising is most likely to reach them. Some of the commoner means of advertising are outlined below.

Local post office or newsagent adverts: Advertising on post office or newsagent notice boards is a simple and effective way of reaching local shoppers. Young mothers drawing their family allowance and senior citizens drawing their pensions almost inevitably use their local post office. The notice board outside, complete with advertisements and parish notices is a focal point for a read and a chat. Most post offices ask for a postcard-size advert (10 cm x 15 cm) and payment is on a weekly basis, in the region of 20p–30p/week. Adverts serve both as an alerting service and as a basic reminder that a farm shop is active.

Parish magazines: Advertising in parish magazines is good value (our local magazines charge about £30–£40 a year for half a page in each of the 12 issues) and helps to support the local community.

Honorary editors are usually most helpful and will make suggestions for improving copy or adding illustrations. Copy is required at least a month before the date of publication.

Other local publications: Look out for publications that fit with your main advertising season, e.g. show or festival brochures, regional 'What's On' guides and amateur dramatic programmes.

In-House magazines and notice boards: It is worth exploring local firms and institutions with a view to advertising in their staff bulletins or on their common room notice boards. The cost is generally reasonable, because benefits are seen as mutual.

Tourist brochures: Advertising in tourist brochures is essential if you live in a holiday area and can sell fresh produce to campers and self-caterers or if you stock gift items. Contact your local Tourist Board for information on publicity—you can find their addresses under 'Tourist Office' in the Yellow Pages.

Local press: The usefulness of the local paper depends largely on the area that it serves in relation to your potential customers. If your shop is conveniently situated at the centre of an area covered by one weekly paper and most of your prospective customers live within that area you are lucky. If customers are scattered over a wider area serviced by a plethora of papers you have a problem.

Advertising in the local press is not cheap (a 7 cm x 4 cm advert in our local paper costs £28, larger adverts *pro rata*), so it is worth shopping around before deciding where to advertise. Ask the advertising manager of your local papers for details of area coverage and circulation. Find out if the paper has different editions for various sub-areas so that you can target your advertising to specific areas; conversely, find out whether you can get reduced rates if you advertise in all the papers of a publishing group.

Advertising space is best used for regular small adverts to alert customers of produce availability. Occasional large displays are useful for attracting new customers but they are expensive. During the fruit season we like to maintain a weekly 'alerting advert' in one of several possible papers in our area rather than to spread our advertising haphazardly over a number of papers. Our reasoning is that it is better to inform some of the customers all of the time than all of the customers some of the time.

Remember that your local press also provides good opportunities for free publicity. Feed your local paper with press releases, invite the farm correspondent to activities on the farm. Send in photos of anything that is news-worthy—animals and children have particular appeal. (See under Public Relations.)

Leaflets: Distribution of leaflets direct to householders tells customers of your existence and of goods in season. You can add comprehensive information such as:

* Location of farm and directions for reaching it.
* Produce grown and when available.
* Your specialities.
* Facilities and special attractions on the farm.
* Other attractions in the neighbourhood.
* Dates and details of any special events.
* Opening times and telephone number for further information.

The back of the leaflets can be used to give recipes. Many housewifes save recipes and will therefore have the telephone number of your farm handy at all times.

Distribution of leaflets is best done in conjunction with the newspaper rounds—see your local newsagent for details. The cost of delivery is at present (1988) about 1½p per leaflet. The Post Office has a Direct Mail distribution system with reduced rates on offer for first-time users. This could be useful if you sell high-value produce and have built up a mailing list, but it is more expensive than newsagent distribution of leaflets. For details of the Post Office scheme write to The Post Office Direct Marketing Section, Headquarters Building, 33 Grosvenor Place, London SW1X 1PX.

Keep a few leaflets for spot distribution to areas of newly constructed housing. This takes time but reaches families who are new to the area, who do not yet grow their own produce and who are likely to be looking for 'somewhere to take the children'.

Layout of leaflets is all-important. Many small printers will advise. It is probably worth paying for professional help from a designer or typographer. A leaflet must combine the eye-catching (so it does not land straight in the bin) with the informative (so it gains a place on the kitchen notice board).

The cost per leaflet decreases with increasing print run, e.g. 3.2p; 2.0p and 1.9p for print runs of 1,000; 5,000 and 10,000 respectively (for black print on coloured A4 paper at 1988 prices).

One of the problems of advertising lies in the difficulty of gauging the response. Leaflets are an exception. Offering the customer a discount on presentation of the leaflet by a certain date allows you to assess the response.

Newsletters: Larger farm shops put out a monthly newsletter during the main season, giving details of forthcoming events, goods in season, special buys, produce information, recipes and competitions. This is a useful means of advertising and a lively way of keeping you and your customers on your toes.

Radio and TV advertising: Radio and TV advertising are expensive and likely to be out of reach of the individual small shop but feasible for joint action for generic advertising. Soft fruit growers in some areas club together to advertise the start of the strawberry and raspberry season. (Chatting to our customers suggests that this is quite an effective alerting service; many housewives do listen to the local radio station.)

Promotions: Promotions aim to lure customers onto your farm and into your shop by enticing them with generous offers of goods or services. In a book entitled *Offensive*

Marketing, Davidson (1975) defines promotions as '. . . *immediate or delayed incentives to purchase, expressed in cash or kind*'.

Examples of promotions used to attract customers to a farm shop include:

* Gifts, such as free jam-jar labels with purchases of fruit, free packs of recipe leaflets, or a free bunch of mint with new potatoes.
* Price reductions such as mid-week discounts, discounts on bulk purchases, reductions for OAPs or for members of group outings.
* Provision of refreshments at favourable prices; some farmers deliberately provide teas as a service rather than as a money-spinning enterprise.
* Promoting farm-based activities (see under Leisure facilities). This can be furthered by organising coach trips, club visits, caravan rallies, open days, produce tasting or cookery demonstrations.

Advertising budget: Information on advertising budgets for farm shops is scant. An advertising expenditure of 1% of farm shop turnover was reported by Thompson (1988).

Advertising expenditure for Mortimer Hill Farm Shop decreased from more than 2% of turnover in the first two years of establishment to an estimated 1% thereafter (the figure is approximate, due to interaction of farm shop and PYO advertising).

By contrast, advertising for PYO tends to be much higher. Advertising for the PYO unit at Marshcroft (Farmers Weekly, 1987) amounted to more than 9% of gross takings in 1986. In a survey of 8 PYO farms in South East England (Jackson & Nicholson, 1985), advertising expenditure varied between 3% and 10% of gross takings.

Advertising expenditure depends on:

* Size of business. Small shops relying largely on local customers do not need wide advertising. Large shops which need to attract customers from further afield are likely to need expensive eye-catching advertisements in a number of papers covering a wide area around the farm.
* Seasonality. Perishable foods with a short harvest season (e.g. strawberries) demand a high level of alerting adverts.
* Age of business. A new enterprise needs much

45

initial advertising. If all goes well, customer loyalty and word of mouth recommendation will take over.

*   Situation. A good site on a busy main road needs less advertising than a remote farm.

Advertising strategy: Do you aim simply to alert the prospective customer of your existence and your goods, or would your shop benefit from more aggressive marketing?

Jackson & Nicholson criticised the advertising on the eight PYO farms surveyed as largely unimaginative: '. . . *the challenge is to create an advertisement which presents the farm and its wares in a different and better light'*. The survey gives an interesting example of one farmer's more thrusting approach to advertising; it begs the question of what is brash and what is effective?

Feedback: Advertising is notoriously difficult. You think you cannot afford it, you know you cannot *not* afford it, and you are never quite sure whether it was worth affording. In a small shop it is easy to chat to customers to find out how they got to hear of you. Formal customer surveys are essential for a large farm shop.

Borrowing

'Banks lend you money as people lend you an umbrella when the sun is shining but want it back when it starts to rain.' Sir Edward Beddington Behrens.

Starting a farm shop can easily push a farmer into the business failure statistics unless the venture is well planned, well integrated into the farm structure and tightly controlled financially. Unless you have retailing experience and boundless confidence start small, using existing farm facilities. Keep capital inputs to an absolute minimum so as to avoid borrowing. Attract customers by the quality of your produce and the warmth of your welcome rather than the plushness of your shop fittings.

If all goes well and the business thrives you will eventually have to invest in improved equipment and larger premises. By this time you will have gained experience in retailing and be familiar with the figures on which to base trading projections and cash flow forecasts for the years ahead.

If you need a loan for expanding your shop, and

you are quite certain that your business warrants it, you will still need to prepare your case carefully:

* Show how the shop business fits into the existing farm economy.
* Show that your financial projections are soundly based on practical understanding of the goods you sell and their market and mark up; customer type and number and average expenditure per customer; present costs of running the shop and the effects of anticipated growth on these costs.
* Show why capital input is needed, how much money you are able to invest, how much you need to borrow, how you plan to repay a loan.
* Show that you are realistic in understanding the limitations of the retail trade, yet quietly confident of your own plans.

If the bank manager does not approve your plans listen carefully to his reasons and, if necessary, re-work your sums. Regard the bank manager as a friend not foe— avoiding failures is of mutual interest. If however you are totally confident that your plans stand up to scrutiny, try another bank or another source of capital. There is no need to feel guilty of disloyalty; relationship with a bank is not a marriage but a working partnership and you must feel free to shop around if you are not happy.

Building control

Building Control concerns the technical aspects of construction which affect the health and safety of people using the building. It deals, for instance, with fire precautions, ventilation, safety of the heating equipment, strength of the structure. Building Control applies both to new buildings and to the conversion of existing premises; it may apply even in cases where planning permission is not required.

Compliance with the building regulations is checked by a Local Authority inspector or by an 'approved inspector' nominated by the person carrying out the work. For details see the *NFU Legal Guide (1987)* or contact your Local Authority.

Buying-in

You would not expect the subject of farm shops to be fraught with emotion but, when it comes to buying-in, passions run high. Those who argue against it are adamant that 'one ill weed mars the whole pot of pottage', that buying-in desecrates the farm shop image, and the farm shop that adds bought-in produce is throwing away not only its own trump card but is spoiling the game for everyone else.

Those in favour of buying-in tend to be fatalistic rather than enthusiastic. As one farmer put it, 'HOME PRODUCE ONLY proved very popular, but not popular enough to tempt away sufficient supermarket customers on a rainy day. That's why we started buying-in'.

The realists admit that it all depends . . . 'There seems to be no recipe for success and there are as many types of big farm shops as there are locations. Some seem to make a reasonable profit selling nothing but their own fruit, fruit juice, coupled with extras like eggs, honey and so on which fit in easily. Others have a carefully planned 12-month operation . . . the majority of items are bought-in and the produce is supported by lines like country handicrafts, home-baked bread, cakes and pastries, jams, pickles and so on. In fact nothing is overlooked which can extract those few more pounds or pennies from the visitor when in a relaxed mood' (Grower Books, 1979).

Reasons for buying-in include the following:

*   Attract customers by providing one-stop-shopping.
*   Fill the gaps when home grown products are not available.
*   Spread the farm shop overheads over a wider range of goods.
*   Add income.
*   Spread income over the year.

One-stop shopping: This sounds simple, but . . . How many lines of products do you reckon you would need to stock in order to compete with a good greengrocer? Have a count up at your local supermarket—the chances are that there will be well upwards of 70 different items at any one time. One-stop shoppers expect to find limes as well as lemons, yellow as well as red and green peppers, watercress at all times (nothing is more perishable and there are 20 in a pack), a wide variety of apples and potatoes and even a choice of onions (Spanish, English, pickling, red, white, shallots and spring onions). You need to be big to carry such stock, or else you will have horrendous wastage.

Filling the gaps: Can you fill gaps in the continuity of home grown produce by buying in good local produce? If not, you will have to buy from the wholesale market or from secondary wholesalers; produce will not be as fresh as your own. Think carefully lest you jeopardise your reputation for freshness. If you do buy-in, make sure all produce is clearly marked 'home-grown' or 'locally grown' or labelled with country of origin.

Spreading the overheads: Widening the range of goods spreads the overheads, but this advantage may be partly offset by additional costs such as rates and transport.

Extra income: Do your sums carefully. Buying-in on a small scale, to supplement your own produce and make use of existing labour and buildings is likely to be profitable. A large scale operation can also pay its way. Beware of the shop which is large enough to attract all the overheads but too small to benefit from economy of scale (see The Trap in Chapter 1).

Spread of income over the year: Make sure that winter losses do not eat up the profits from the summer trading! (see under Mortimer Hill Farm Shop—a case study).

Summary: Buying-in allows you to maximise the use of existing facilities. If your shop is open and at the ready, and if space and staff are not fully occupied then bought-in goods make sense. Beware of staying open specifically for the sale of bought-in goods unless you are sure you can reach a high level of sales.

Capital inputs

The capital needed for setting up a farm shop depends on what buildings and facilities you have, what you want, what you can afford, and how much of the work you can do yourself.

It is advisable to start modestly with a small shop located in an existing building and allow trade to build up gradually. Building a new farm shop or even conversion of existing buildings can be extremely expensive and is best delayed until you are certain that trade warrants it.

It is impossible to generalise about the capital needed to set up a shop. To estimate the order of magnitude make a checklist of your likely needs and work your way through it, trying to put a figure to each item—then add a generous allowance for the unforeseen. Your list should take into account:

*   Access and amenity.
  > Access from highway.
  > Upgrading of farm road to the shop.
  > Parking.
  > Landscaping.
  > Leisure facilities.
*   Signposts.
*   Buildings.
  > Cost of planning applications, architectural and technical advice.
  > Building costs for the farm shop.
  > Building costs for working area, storage area and access between these areas.
  > Toilets and washing facilities.
  > Cool stores if needed.
*   Services.
  > Electricity.
  > Plumbing.
*   Heating.
*   Security.
*   Painting and decorating.
*   Equipment.
  > Scales and cash registers.
  > Shelves and counters.
  > Freezers and coolers.
  > Telephone and answerphone.
  > Minor items such as price markers, bag dispensers, bag sealers, storage containers, cleaning equipment.

An example of capital inputs to develop a farm shop is given in Table 6. In this example the site had good access and parking, the building was attractive but needed re-roofing. Over a six-year period the shop was built up to a size capable of handling annual sales of £100,000 of home-grown and bought-in produce (mainly fruit and vegetables) and it also served as the sales point for PYO soft fruit. Investments totalled almost £12,000 with an average of about £3,000 in each of the first three years and about £1,000 per year thereafter (see also Cash flow).

Table 6. Developing a farm shop. Capital inputs 1981–1987

1.	Improvement of farm drive	£ 600
	Landscaping	£ 800
	Play area/picnic area	£ 1,000
2.	Signposts[1]	£ 200
3.	Buildings re-roofing	£ 2,500
	doors	£ 500
	internal work	£ 700
	toilets[1]	£ 1,600
4.	Electricity	£ 500
5.	Security	£ 300
6.	Equipment scales[2]	£ 950
	tills[3]	£ 315
	shelving	£ 500
	telephone & answerphone	£ 200
	cooler & freezer[4]	£ 700
	other	£ 300
	TOTAL	£11,665

Say £12,000 written off over 10 years @ 12%

Thus annual charge for capital inputs = £2,124[5]

Based on Mortimer Hill, 1981–87.

(1) Own labour used.
(2) One second-hand fan-scale; one new electronic scale, and two second hand ones.
(3) One old mechanical cash register, two second-hand electronic tills.
(4) Second hand.
(5) Throughout this book the annual charge method is used in order to take account of both capital repayment and interest. The annual charge for an input of £12,000 written off over 10 years at 12% is 12 x £177 (see amortization table) = £2,124.

Repayments of capital and interest. Amortization Table

Annual charge to write off £1,000.

Write-off Period (Years)	Rate of Interest												
	8%	10%	11%	12%	13%	14%	15%	16%	17%	18%	19%	20%	25%
5	251	264	271	278	284	291	299	305	313	320	327	334	373
6	216	230	237	243	250	257	265	271	279	286	293	301	339
7	192	206	212	219	226	233	240	248	255	262	270	278	316
8	174	188	194	202	208	216	223	230	238	245	253	261	301
10	149	163	170	177	184	192	200	207	215	223	231	239	280
12	133	147	154	162	169	177	185	192	201	209	217	226	269
15	117	132	139	147	155	163	171	179	188	196	205	214	260
20	102	117	126	134	142	151	160	168	178	187	196	205	253
25	94	110	119	128	136	146	155	164	173	183	193	202	252
30	89	106	113	124	133	143	153	161	172	181	191	202	251
40	84	102	111	121	131	141	150	160	170	180	190	200	250

Cash flow

Capital inputs into a farm shop are not spread evenly over the years (see under Capital inputs). Setting up a business demands an initial capital input for preparing the premises and for equipping the shop; thereafter the expenses generally level off until eventually the facilities are outgrown and another burst of spending is required (see under Scale of operation).

Financial planning must take account of these variations. A cash flow is a projection of the flow of money into and out of a business over a period of time. A simple example of a cash flow projection is given in Table 7. It is based on a capital input of £12,000 spread over a six year period, with £3,000 spent in each of the first three years and £1,000 in each subsequent year. Shop sales increase from £25,000 in the first year of operation to £104,000 in the sixth year. Wages and running costs increase slowly at first (while a high proportion of family labour is used) and then more rapidly.

The figures show that the cumulative balance is negative for the first three years of operation; the shop begins to 'pay back' only in its fourth year.

Cash flow projections can be made on a monthly basis (to identify the seasonal periods in which peak borrowing may occur) or on an annual basis, as above to assess the time taken for investments in a business to be paid back. Cash flow projections are particularly important in the case of a business which develops only very gradually, e.g. growing top fruit specifically for sale in a farm shop. For examples of cash flows in horticulture see ADAS (1984).

Table 7. Cash flow calculation for a farm shop[1]

		1	2	3	4	5	6
							Year of operation
SALES	(£000/yr)						
Shop sales (s)		25	36	52	78	95	104
COSTS	(£000/yr)						
Produce for resale		18	26	38	57	69	76
Running costs		8	9	10	14	16	18
Capital inputs		3	3	3	1	1	1
Total costs (c)		29	38	51	72	86	95
Net cash flow (s−c)		−4	−2	1	6	9	9
Cumulative Balance[2]		−4	−6	−5	+1	+10	+19

Notes: 1. No allowance made for inflation.
2. This is the bank balance at the end of the year. No allowance has been made for interest charge on negative balances.

Complaints

'If we please you tell your friends. If not please tell us'

Complaints are valuable. Treat them with respect and gratitude. The drill for dealing with complaints is: listen; thank and reply; action; follow-up.

Listen: Most customers dislike complaining. They are generally uneasy, wait until you are not busy, take you aside and open with *'I hate to complain—but . . .'*. Listen carefully and question gently.

Reply: Thank your customer for taking the trouble to complain. A customer who makes the effort to return to your shop to point out to you a speck of mould on the top of a jar of jam is doing you a favour. So long as people complain it shows they care; you have only minor problems. If they do not bother to complain and simply shop elsewhere you have a major problem and may not even be aware of it!

Mistakes happen in any business and frankness is usually appreciated. If you know what went wrong, give your customer a brief explanation. If not, promise to investigate.

Action: Exchange the goods or give a refund. If in real doubt, take the name and address of the customer, investigate and keep him or her informed.

Follow-up: If stock is suspect, get rid of it and trace back to find out what went wrong. Keep a complaints book. It will impress your customers and provide marvellous reading in the years to come.

Complaints about money: It is no sin to make a mistake; it is a sin to handle a mistake badly. Train yourself and your staff to apologize and to rectify mistakes without fuss and with good grace. To minimise mistakes:

* Develop a feel for the order of magnitude of a sale. Does the look of the basketful of goods tally with the sum rung up on the till? If not, play safe and check.
* Encourage customers to take the receipt slip.
* Keep bank notes on the till or clipped to the till until the customer has checked the change.
* Reconcile cash in the till against till statements daily, and note any discrepancies.

Complaints about goods: Complaints about home-grown produce are rare. Where they do occur take them seriously and investigate.

Bought-in goods cause more problems. Apples that look perfect when you open the pack develop brown pitting within some days because they have been taken from the cold store too abruptly. Potatoes that look fine when you buy them turn out to be frosted—but this will not show up for some days. Celery which looks perfect on the outside may be slimy from the inside. The variations are endless. Apologise, offer a refund or exchange, and report back to source. (Wholesalers ask for complaints to be made within 24 hours of purchase: make a habit of checking goods on receipt. If problems crop up later, notify your supplier as soon as you can. Most wholesalers will treat your complaints fairly.)

Customer profiles: *'The customer is always right.'* Well nearly always, but often enough to justify a policy of erring on the side of generosity when dealing with complaints. Ask your customers to notify you of any problems and to return defective produce to you as soon as possible so that you can investigate rapidly and remove other produce of the same batch.

The customer is sometimes wrong but even if you are 99% certain that his complaint is not justified do not tell him so—there is always that lingering doubt . . . listen, and investigate. Whether you offer an immediate refund or exchange depends on circumstances. It is generally better to do so, making it clear that you always like to give the benefit of the doubt.

A few people, luckily only a very few, are endemic complainers. They are easy to spot. They happen only when the shop is full and you are extremely busy. They launch into full spate and continue until they eventually talk themselves to a standstill. Avoid questioning or arguing —it re-opens the floodgates. The best strategy is a quiet word of thanks then—quickly before the surprise effect is lost—deal with the complaint rapidly and firmly.

Consumer rights and protection

The *Sales of Goods Act 1979* sets out the basic legal rules concerning the sale of goods, stipulating, for instance, that goods sold by description must match that description and that goods must be of merchantable quality. The *Unfair Contract Terms Act 1977* restricts the sellers right to contract out of the conditions governing the sales of goods. The effect is that '*a customer who buys defective food or other goods on a direct sale usually has a contractual right to complain and obtain redress. Normally the customer returns the defective goods and is refunded the price or given replacement goods*'. (NFU Legal Guide, 1987.)

The *Consumer Protection Act (1987)* covers consumer safety. It applies to processed goods rather than to primary agricultural produce, imposing strict liability on the producer for defects in produce which cause damage to consumers.

Credit

'*In God we trust. All others pay cash.*'

Credit sales create bookwork, hassle and cash-flow problems. Avoid them.

Disabled customers

Building regulations oblige you to provide access for the disabled if you   are building new farm shop premises. There is no such obligation if you are converting an existing farm building into a farm shop. Nevertheless, it is well worthwhile to do so if possible. The disabled also need access to toilets. Reserve a parking place for disabled drivers close to the shop.

Display of goods

'*The first bite is taken with the eye—70% of all messages are visual.*' (Bill Webb, on Shop Design.)

Learning to display goods effectively is half the fun and the art of shopkeeping. The best way to learn is by example —a successful barrow boy can teach you much about the use of colour, texture and shape and how to make an attractive display of goods. Browse around the supermarkets too to see examples of effective display. Add commonsense and constant vigil to ensure that produce is fresh, that sub-standard produce is removed at regular intervals, and shelves are kept topped up.

Home-made produce displayed at table height is difficult to resist.

Good lighting is vital. A combination of background lighting and spot lighting gives maximum flexibility. Bear in mind the quality as well as the intensity of the light—tomatoes for instance appear to change colour as they are moved from sunlight to tungsten to fluorescent light. Consult your electrician or a lighting expert to guide you as to the best light for effective display of your type of produce.

Customers appreciate convenience when they shop. The easier it is to reach, touch, smell and inspect the produce the more likely it is to sell itself. Avoid displaying goods above eye level or below knee level; tables or counters 36—40 inches (1 metre) high and shelving 3—5 feet (1—1.7 metres) high are the prime display levels. It is best to have low surfaces in the central area of a shop, with taller displays and higher shelves on the outer walls.

Disperse high-demand items and specialities throughout the sales area so as to attract customers to all parts of the shop. Essentials such as potatoes are best displayed near the furthest point of the sales area so that customers are drawn past the other goods. Items for impulse buying are generally displayed near the high-demand items and near the checkout.

Diversification

'If we who can diversify do, then all will benefit from reduced surpluses.' Hew Watt, 1988.

Alternative farm enterprises, from farm walks to wargames, snail-farming to craft products, are no longer the domain of the farming cranks. Diversification is in vogue. The farming press is full of articles on diversification, giving details of planning and of case histories of unusual farm ventures. The subject is fully explored in an excellent book on alternative enterprises (Slee, 1987).

     Reasons for diversification include:
* Extra income needed now.
* Extra income needed in the future.
* Uneasy about the future of farming and too many eggs in one basket.
* Diversification is in fashion.
* Grants available (see Diversification Grants).
* Looking for a challenge.
* Looking for a use for surplus land, labour or produce.

Which of the above are valid for you? Surplus land, labour and enthusiasm for dealing with people are real assets. Fashion and the availability of grants should not be deciding factors! Sift through the alternatives which appeal to you. Avoid 'just drifting' into a farm shop. Marketing requires entrepreneurial skills very different from farming skills.

Diversification grants

From January 1st 1988 financial assistance for diversification became available through the *Farm Diversification Grant Scheme*. Capital investments eligible for grant aid include on-farm tourism, craft workshops, visitor attractions, sport and recreational facilities, value-added processing of food and other produce, PYO, and farm shops. Grants are payable to farmers who earn at least half their income from farming, have been in farming for at least five years (or hold a suitable training certificate) and spend at least 1100 hours per year working on the holding. Suitably qualified farmers under the age of 40 are eligible for 31.25% grant, over 40's receive 25% of the cost of the new enterprise, and the total investment on each farm must not exceed £35,000 in the first six years of the scheme.

The grant regulations (MAFF, 1987) apply to *'a shop which is not a normal retail outlet but covers farm shops in which the majority of the produce sold has been produced on the holding. This includes non-agricultural goods (e.g. craft items, tourist souvenirs, prepared foods) produced on the holding.'* The grant-aid applies to work such as standard permanent fixtures and fittings but not to moveable equipment such as refrigerators or cash registers.

Applicants are asked to submit investment plans and profit forecasts for the new enterprise. Full details and application forms are available from your local MAFF office. ADAS is offering initial free advice on general questions and can put you in touch with other relevant organisations in your area. Further detailed advice or feasibility studies are chargeable.

Preliminary data on uptake of Diversification Grants (Farm Development Review, 1988) showed that of 708 applications submitted to the MAFF during the first seven months of the scheme, 62 related to farm shops selling food, 19 to farm shops selling other goods and 19 to new pick-your-own ventures i.e. more than 13% of all applications involved retailing from the farm.

Grants for feasibility studies and for marketing: Grants to help with the cost of carrying out a feasibility study for a new farm activity or to plan the marketing for a new venture were introduced on 1st August, 1988 (MAFF 1988). Feasibility studies aim to assess the potential for a new product or service, the necessary inputs of capital and labour, and interactions with the existing farm business. The consultant who carries out the feasibility study must be a member of a recognised body such as the Institute of Marketing, the British Institute of Agricultural Consultants, ADAS, Agricultural Colleges or the Royal Institute of Chartered Surveyors. The rate of grant for a feasibility study is 50% of cost, up to a maximum grant of £3000 for a single business or £10,000 for a group of businesses.

Marketing grants are designed to encourage better marketing; such grants cover a part of the expense of employing qualified marketing personnel to study the marketing of new products or services. Marketing plans must include an estimate of the quantity and value of the proposed product over a 3-year period. Grants are paid at the rate of 40%, 30% and 20% of marketing expenses for the first, second and third year of marketing respectively, up to a maximum of £3000 per year for a single business or £10,000 a year for a group.

Full details of both schemes are given in a booklet *(FDS 3)* available free from ADAS offices.

Dogs

Make sure you have a firm policy on dogs—and that you stick to it. There should definitely be no dogs in the farm shop. Outdoors, you can be a little more flexible—'Please keep dogs *ON* the lead and *OFF* the crops' is a good compromise to satisfy dog-owners and dog-haters. Make sure you have a few tethering posts outside the shop, otherwise you effectively allow dog-walkers access to the farm without allowing them to spend their money in your shop.

A simple tethering post.

Equipment

Scales: The most basic shop equipment is a set of scales. Kitchen scales will not do!

Fan scales are useful for a small business or when starting up. They are easy to use and are still available second-hand, but be careful to check that they meet the necessary standards of accuracy demanded by the Weights and Measures Authority. If fan scales go wrong be sure to ask for an estimate for the repair before committing yourself—the cost of fixing what is now outdated equipment may exceed the cost of another second-hand set of scales.

Electronic scales have superseded the fan scale. They are very quick and easy to use and show the customer exactly what is happening. Their use eliminates the problem of 'reading up or reading down' when the marker on the fan scale falls between two units. Assuming you have always 'read down' on the fan scale (to give the customer the benefit of the doubt of the 1p more or less) then for every 100 items sold, some 50 would have been 'read down'. The saving of ½p per item sold soon adds up, and makes a convincing argument for investing in electronic scales.

Disadvantages of electronic scales are dependence on power points and extreme sensitivity to draughts. Also, they are expensive; a new set of scales costs upwards of £500. Second-hand equipment can sometimes be found (look out for a shop or a supermarket going out of business). You need a spare set of scales at the ready to meet a sudden rush, to cut out panics when a scale hiccups, and to avoid expensive service contracts. Once you have used electronic scales you will never want to go back to the old fan scale but keep a set in case of power cuts.

Cash Registers: Cash registers are in effect a combined adding machine and money box. They are highly convenient but you can make do without them when you first set up shop. On a pin-money scale simply use mental arithmetic and your pocket.

The next stage up is a calculator and a cash box while you hunt out an old-fashioned mechanical cash register. These old workhorses are cumbersome and slower to operate than a calculator. Nevertheless, they do, at a decent human pace, most things that a small shop is likely to want

Fan scales (left) are an inexpensive way of equipping a small shop, and a useful back-up in case of power cuts. Electronic scales (right) are easy to use; enter the price per lb and the scales will show the total price.

to do i.e. register individual sales, add up sales, code and add groups of sales, give totals and print-outs. Mechanical cash registers are robust but once the motor fails it is probably cheaper to scrap them rather than repair them. (Our £15 machine worked like a Trojan for two years until we went electronic; it still serves as our 'insurance back-up'.)

Electronic tills are a joy to use. Unless you are gadget crazy, go for the simpler heavy-duty machines (£400 and upwards). Make sure though that you have the possibility of coding sales into as many groups as you will need for farm records analysis (sales of each of the major crops sold through the farm shop), and for farm shop analysis (sales of the major classes of bought-in produce) and for VAT-rated goods.

Power cuts: Electricity cuts cause chaos in the modern shop: immobilized scales and tills bring business to a standstill. It is therefore worth having a battery-operated option on equipment, or keeping an old set of fan scales and a money box at the ready. Also, make sure you know how to open the electronic till manually or you risk being locked out of your change.

Equipment insurance: You will probably be offered service contracts on farm shop equipment such as scales, tills and freezers. This can be an expensive safeguard so do your sums carefully.

New equipment is under guarantee for at least a year. Following the guarantee period, risks are small for some years (modern electronic equipment gives little trouble in the first few years of life) so it is arguable whether insurance is worthwhile. By the time the equipment is old and liable to give trouble the cost of a service contract is likely to be prohibitive. The alternative is to have a back-up of spare second-hand equipment. It is probably cheaper to have a spare deep freeze at the ready than to pay for the insurance of freezer and contents. A second-hand chest freezer is not expensive to buy, gives a good feeling of security, and comes in useful when defrosting. Similarly, keep a spare set of scales and an old cash register at the ready to meet a sudden emergency and to obviate the need for expensive service contracts.

Family planning

If you are thinking of starting a farm shop do your planning as a family. A retail enterprise is likely to involve the skills of both husband and wife and to impinge on the privacy of family and farm. Do not contemplate taking on a farm shop without the approval and enthusiasm of your partner. If you have, or hope to have a family, consider a joint approach to farm shop planning and family planning! Young shops and young children have much in common; both involve long hours, both make urgent demands on your time, both involve a myriad of two-minute jobs rather than organised lumps of work you can readily delegate. If you have been up with a screaming child half the night you will find it difficult to cope with a tiresome customer during the day.

The best time for setting up a shop is before you have a family or after the children are past the most demanding stages. (Our children were 16 and 14 when we launched into PYO and farm shop enterprise; we had no torn loyalties and no regrets. We found unexpected advantages; the children were old enough to join in the fun and occasional pain of a growing business; they and their friends benefitted from the seasonal employment possibilities;

they threw in their considerable skills and energies at times of crisis; they enjoyed our 'less-than-tidy' home and they benefitted from lack of parental fuss as they took their teenage steps towards independence.)

Finance

Chapter 1 looks at the costs of farm retailing from enterprises varying in size and in product range. Other sections relating to finance include:
Accounts; Borrowing; Capital costs; Cash flow; Credit; Diversification Grants; Mark-up and margins; Records; Retail statistics; Running costs; VAT.

Food statistics

'We are, literally, what we eat.' Terence Stamp.

How much do we eat, what do we eat and how much do we pay for it? The *National Food Survey* gives annual statistics which are useful background information for the farmer/retailer.

Expenditure on food and drink in the UK reached almost £59 billion in 1986, accounting for about 25% of total consumers' expenditure (see Figure 8). Household food purchases accounted for about 55% of the total expenditure on food and drink (see Figure 9). Weekly food expenditure per person averaged just under £10 in 1986; the most expensive item in the budget was meat (£2.85), followed by fruit and vegetables (£1.98). Expenditure on milk and cream was £1.04, and on eggs about 20p. Figure 10 shows the composition of the average 'shopping bag'. The detailed statistics are given in Tables 8–11.

These figures are, of course, the mid-point of a very wide range; some families spend a lot of money on fresh produce, others appear to live almost exclusively on convenience foods. The *National Food Survey* adds information on eating habits in relation to region, family structure, household size, age and affluence. For instance, one adult living alone is likely, on average, to spend twice as much per head on fresh fruit as a family of two adults and three children (see Figure 11). This is worth knowing if you are in the fruit trade—woo your single customers! Regional variations give food for thought: does the low consumption of fresh greens in Scotland (see Figure 12) indicate that the Scots do not like greens (so there is little point in growing them) or does it indicate that the market is not well supplied so it would be wise to grow them for your farm shop? Local observation will have to guide you. Note particularly the income groups in your area—you can easily upset the statistics by tempting customers with freshly picked asparagus or mange-tout or other exotics if you farm in Home-County 'Yuppie-land'; this will be more difficult in a less affluent area.

Despite their obvious limitations, the statistics are useful at the initial planning stage when deciding whether or not to opt for a farm shop. Assume, initially, that you are dealing with the 'average' consumer. The statistics show how much this mythical average consumer spends on the type of goods you hope to sell. Set your target turnover. You can then work out the number of customers you will need to achieve your target. Relate this back to your local conditions (location of farm, size and character of population of the surrounding area and competition) to weigh up whether your project is feasible.

Suppose you are thinking of setting up a farm shop for the sale of meat and eggs. Your reckoning would be:

* Average weekly consumer expenditure (1986 figures).

Meat	£2.85
Eggs	£0.20
Total	£3.05

* Target turnover: Assume you are aiming at a level of turnover equivalent to that of the High Street butcher. This was £127,685 for 1984; (see Retail statistics); assuming it is 15% higher by 1986, brings the target figure to £146,837 per year.

* Number of customers: To achieve this target requires the following number of customers:

  146,837 ÷ 3.05 = 48,143/year = 926/week

* Evaluation: Suppose your farm is near a village of 2,000 inhabitants; you would need almost 50% up-take of your services to achieve your target. Is this possible? Only if your shop is easily accessible to a carnivorous population, if there is no butcher in the village, and your nearest shopping centre is many inaccessible miles away.

If your farm is located within easy reach of a town of 200,000 people you would need only a 5% up-take of your services. The questions to consider are:

* Where is the competition? Are you filling an obvious gap in the market or will you have to gain customers from existing competition?
* What is the quality of the competition?
* What specialities and attractions can you offer that will give you an advantage over your competitors? Why should people desert the convenience of the shopping centre to come down your farm drive?

Figure 8.
Consumer expenditure in the UK 1986

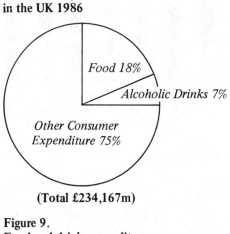

(Total £234,167m)

Figure 9.
Food and drink expenditure in the UK 1986

(Total £58,902m)

Figure 10.
The average weekly shopping bag, 1986

(Total £9.87 per head per week)

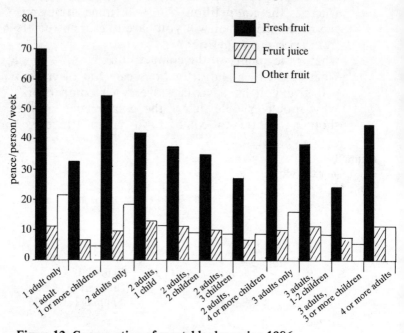

Figure 11. Expenditure on fruit by houshold composition 1986

Legend:
- Fresh fruit
- Fruit juice
- Other fruit

y-axis: pence/person/week

x-axis categories:
1 adult only; 1 adult 1 or more children; 2 adults only; 2 adults, 1 child; 2 adults, 2 children; 2 adults, 3 children; 2 adults, 4 or more children; 3 adults only; 3 adults, 1-2 children; 3 adults, 3 or more children; 4 or more adults

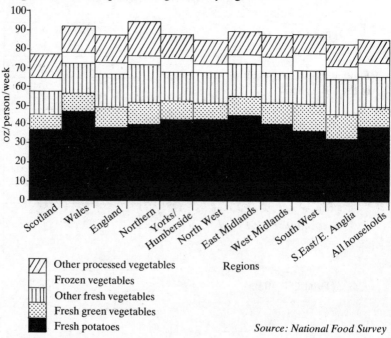

Figure 12. Consumption of vegetables by region 1986

y-axis: oz/person/week

x-axis categories:
Scotland; Wales; England; Northern; Yorks/ Humberside; North West; East Midlands; West Midlands; South West; S.East/E. Anglia; All households

Regions

Legend:
- Other processed vegetables
- Frozen vegetables
- Other fresh vegetables
- Fresh green vegetables
- Fresh potatoes

Source: National Food Survey

Table 8. Consumers' expenditure in the United Kingdom

	1976 £m	1976 %	1981 £m	1981 %	1986 £m	1986 %
Household expenditure on food	13,941	18.4	24,207	15.8	32,342	13.8
Expenditure on meals out	3,151	4.2	6,285	4.1	10,086	4.3
Total expenditure on food	17,092	22.5	30,492	19.9	42,428	18.1
Alcoholic drink	5,714	7.5	11,152	7.3	16,474	7.0
Total food and drink	22,806	30.1	41,644	27.2	58,902	25.2
Total consumers' expenditure	75,873	100.0	153,027	100.0	234,167	100.0

Source: National Food Survey

Table 9. Consumption and expenditure for main food groups
(per person per week)

	Consumption 1984	Consumption 1985	Consumption 1986	Expenditure 1984	Expenditure 1985	Expenditure 1986
	(ounces) (a)			(pence)		
Milk and cream (pints)	4.31	4.13	4.15	96.16	98.66	103.85
Cheese	3.84	3.91	4.16	29.13	31.32	33.91
Meat and meat products	36.60	36.77	37.08	261.97	273.51	284.59
Fish	4.89	4.90	5.16	40.77	44.54	50.41
Eggs (no)	3.21	3.15	3.01	20.99	21.10	20.24
Fats and oils	10.29	10.07	10.49	35.47	36.77	36.15
Sugar and preserves	11.10	10.27	10.03	18.45	17.36	17.57
Fruit and vegetables	110.69	111.99	117.07	169.40	173.43	197.64
Cereals (inc. bread)	54.03	53.84	54.94	136.93	144.12	159.76
Beverages	2.76	2.70	2.76	38.32	41.57	43.61
Other foods	–	–	–	33.49	35.02	38.96
All foods	–	–	–	£8.81	£9.17	£9.87

(a) except where otherwise stated   *Source: National Food Survey*

Table 10. Consumption and expenditure for vegetables and fruit
(per person per week)

	Consumption 1984	Consumption 1985	Consumption 1986	Expenditure 1984	Expenditure 1985	Expenditure 1986
	(ounces)			(pence)		
VEGETABLES:						
Potatoes	39.82	40.96	38.76	25.00	17.62	21.41
Fresh green	10.83	9.78	11.11	13.92	14.46	16.47
Other fresh	15.26	15.70	16.82	28.77	30.60	34.99
Frozen, including vegetable products	5.19	5.97	6.28	12.98	14.23	15.29
Other processed, including vegetable products	11.75	12.51	13.28	32.27	36.13	39.40
Total vegetables	82.84	84.93	86.27	112.95	113.04	127.57
FRUIT:						
Fresh	18.99	18.52	20.33	36.33	38.82	45.56
Fruit juices	5.28	5.21	6.84	8.39	9.62	11.22
Other fruit products	3.58	3.33	3.63	11.75	11.96	13.29
Total fruit	27.85	27.06	30.80	56.45	60.39	70.07

Source: National Food Survey

Table 11. Seasonal purchases and consumption of eggs, vegetables & fruit 1986 (oz per person per week, except where otherwise stated)

	Consumption[1]					Purchases	Percentage of all households purchasing each type of food during Survey week
	Jan/March	April/June	July/Sept	Oct/Dec	Yearly average	Yearly average	
EGGS (no)	3.05	3.23	2.85	2.90	3.01	2.91	62
VEGETABLES:							
Fresh							
Old potatoes							
January-August							
not prepacked	35.03	21.00	0.97	⋯	14.25	13.68	
prepacked	6.57	5.74	0.35	⋯	3.16	3.16	
New potatoes							
January-August							na.
not prepacked	0.71	8.15	22.10	⋯	7.74	7.03	
prepacked	0.07	0.82	3.39	⋯	1.07	1.07	
Potatoes							
Sept-Dec							
not prepacked	⋯	⋯	6.87	32.57	9.86	8.89	
prepacked	⋯	⋯	2.11	8.62	2.68	2.68	
Total potatoes	42.38	35.70	35.78	41.19	38.76	36.52	62
Cabbages	3.89	3.71	3.59	3.33	3.63	3.02	27
Brussels sprouts	2.21	0.35	0.26	2.78	1.40	1.22	15
Cauliflowers	1.00	2.80	3.27	3.36	2.61	2.46	21
Leafy salads	0.78	2.07	2.59	1.21	1.66	1.49	34
Peas	0.31	0.21	0.87	0.37	0.44	0.14	1
Beans	0.46	0.36	2.36	0.86	1.01	0.22	3
Other green veg	0.31	0.40	0.37	0.34	0.36	0.27	5
Total fresh green veg	8.96	9.90	13.32	12.24	11.11	8.81	65
Carrots	4.69	3.39	3.79	4.30	4.04	3.66	39
Turnips & swedes	1.50	0.71	0.51	1.77	1.12	1.02	11
Other root veg	0.95	0.68	0.67	0.97	0.82	0.64	10
Onions, shallots, leeks	3.64	3.33	3.31	3.65	3.48	3.11	39
Cucumbers	0.63	1.32	1.63	0.86	1.11	1.04	25
Mushrooms	0.94	0.93	0.84	0.83	0.89	0.88	28
Tomatoes	2.44	3.91	5.30	3.44	3.77	3.22	49
Miscellaneous veg	1.16	1.36	2.32	1.49	1.58	1.42	20
Total other veg	15.95	15.63	18.37	17.31	16.82	14.99	79
FRUIT: Fresh							
Oranges	3.85	4.43	2.23	1.87	3.10	3.09	25
Other citrus fruit	2.89	1.33	1.02	2.64	1.97	1.97	20
Apples	7.13	7.52	6.49	7.89	7.26	6.50	51
Pears	0.99	1.08	0.73	1.32	1.03	0.99	11
Stone fruit	0.23	0.53	3.70	0.38	1.21	1.13	12
Grapes	0.32	0.45	0.84	0.92	0.63	0.63	10
Soft fruit, other than grapes	0.20	0.45	2.72	0.25	0.90	0.49	5
Bananas	2.65	3.22	3.36	3.02	3.06	3.06	36
Rhubarb	0.09	0.96	0.43	0.04	0.38	0.06	1
Other fresh fruit	0.22	0.60	1.81	0.54	0.79	0.79	7
Total fresh fruit	18.57	20.57	23.33	18.86	20.33	18.70	72

1 Includes food eaten outside the home   Source: National Food Survey

Freshness

'Farm-fresh', 'straight from the fields' and 'nature's food' are over-worked terms used in nostalgic back-to-the-farm advertisements, promoting anything from frozen vegetables to steam-baked bread. The advertising industry has been quick to recognise the appeal of the fresh countryside image: yet for processed foods it must surely remain an image?

Asparagus, pick-your-own or picked while you wait. Supermarkets cannot match such freshness.

The undisputed advantage of the farm shop comes in the shape of lettuce dripping with dew, eggs warm from the nest, strawberries picked within minutes (rather than hours or days) of sale, carrots and beetroot with turgid green leaf, plums with the bloom still on them. No supermarket can match such freshness. Nevertheless there is no room for complacency. An hour spent looking around the fruit and vegetable section of one of the better supermarkets is a sobering education. The quality of produce has improved greatly over the last ten years as the multiples have deliberately muscled their way into the greengrocery business.

The demands of the mutiples have dictated changes in the horticultural industry. Multiples tend to by-pass the traditional wholesale markets, preferring to buy direct from larger growers or co-operatives on a contract basis. This means that they can control the entire marketing operation. Perishable goods pass rapidly from harvesting to shop via a cool-chain marketing system based on rapid extraction of field heat and temperature-controlled conditions during storage, transport and in the retail display. Increased speed of marketing has been accompanied by improved packaging, labelling, and display (note especially the quality of the lighting used in the supermarkets).

Nevertheless, a closer look at the cool chain system shows up some snags. The obvious one is expense—to achieve what is simply a fresh looking lettuce on the supermarket shelf has required an enormous back-up of capital expenditure without actually adding anything to the product. Cool storage has yet to overcome technical problems such as condensation. Also, while perishable products look good in the cooling cabinet, they tend to collapse rapidly in the shopping basket or in a warm kitchen. Cool-chain marketing is liable to lull distributors into complacency, believing that produce in the cold store will keep when in fact it is getting stale.

Freshness in the farm shop can and MUST be the linchpin of the operation. Wilted and tired produce must be ruthlessly removed. For perishable crops there can be no compromise. The exception, for higher value items, is to have a totally distinct sales section (Bargain Bin) for 'less than perfect' produce which must be clearly labelled as such e.g. 'Strawberries picked yesterday, so half price' or 'Windfall Bramleys—use within one week of purchase'. This has two advantages. First, it is an attraction for jam-makers and bargain hunters. Second, it gives the implicit assurance that all other strawberries are of today's picking and that Bramleys are of keeping quality.

There are obvious advantages to selling only home-grown produce, for the control of quality and freshness is entirely in your own hands. The addition of bought-in produce brings with it all the problems faced by the smaller greengrocer including the difficulty of getting first-rate quality produce, competition with the cool-chain marketing of the multiples, and the problems of pack size.

Good housekeeping – minimising wastage

'Housekeeping ain't no joke.' Louisa May Alcott, 1865.

The rural setting of a farm shop is an attraction in fine weather; in wet weather it can be a disaster. However careful you are to take the weather forecast into consideration when harvesting or buying fresh produce for the shop, you will make mistakes. There will be times when you fill the shelves with optimism but the skies cloud over and you get landed. You cannot hope to avoid this, the best you can do is to take certain measures to minimize it:

*   Harvest produce on a 'little and often' basis, even at the cost of efficiency.
*   Do not be tempted by special discounts on quantity purchases. It is better to underbuy, even at the risk of having to top-up with produce from more expensive sources.
*   Find out what you can and cannot store with impunity. Consider the costs and benefits of a cool store. Take time to look round greengroceries and to assess the commonest casualties—flabby parsnips, wilted watercress, sprouted onions, and limp leeks are sober warnings of what to avoid.
*   Be scrupulously careful with stock rotation to ensure that goods are used in order of purchase.
*   Take care in topping up the shelves in a self-service shop to avoid throwing new produce over the remnants of the previous batch.

Feeding surplus produce to livestock reduces the agony of the inevitable wastage.

* Withdraw less-than-perfect goods before they go 'sad' or bad. Throw out ruthlessly. Feeding waste to pigs or goats helps to lessen the agony.

* A bargain bin is worth considering if you are sure that this will boost total sales and will neither blurr your farm-fresh image nor reduce the sale of full-price produce. Suppose, for example, you have over-bought cauliflowers. What will you do with them? (They are three days old, bought-in at 40p (£4.80 for a crate of 12) and retailing at 60p.) Assess the following options:

  'Make 'em eat 'em' philosophy. Keep the caulis on the shelf at 60p until they sell or rot. (Possible gain is £2.40 per crate, possible loss to trade and image is inestimable.)

  'Cut your losses quick' philosophy. Throw away the old stock and buy new. (Loss of £4.80 per crate could be recouped by the sale of two crates of fresh produce.)

  'Good housekeeping solution'. Put the old stock on the shelf clearly labelled 'Reduced for quick sale— 30p'. At the same time, put out fresh produce at 60p. (You will lose £1.20 per crate on the old stock but give customers a good buy. Loss of image and of trade is avoided as customers have the choice of goods.)

Summary: Wastage is a problem in any shop, and particularly when dealing with perishable goods such as fruit and vegetables. Try to minimise wastage but accept that a certain amount is unavoidable. It is better to throw away produce than to throw away your reputation for freshness.

Growing fruit and vegetables for the shop

Most farm shops start as an adjunct to an existing farm activity, selling farm produce which would otherwise flow through the conventional marketing channels. Does it make sense to diversify the range of farm activities specifically to supply a farm shop? To answer this question you need to know how much produce would be needed, and to calculate the areas involved.

Rough estimates (see Table 12) suggest that producing a range of seven of the commoner summer vegetables for a shop serving 1000 customers per week takes less than two acres of land. Almost one acre is for potatoes; cauliflowers and lettuce each require about a quarter of an acre; carrots, cabbage, onions and peas require about one tenth of an acre each.

Although the areas required are only small, the organisational problems of growing this diversity of crops are large. More specifically:

* A high level of horticultural expertise is needed to cover a wide range of crops.
* A high level of organisation is needed to ensure that each crop gets proper attention as and when needed.
* Inputs of labour and machinery requirements are high in relation to the area of the plots.
* Much skill, and considerable luck with the weather, are needed to achieve continuity of supply. A succession of crops over the 13—week period means sowing or planting very small areas at a time, and makes for great complexity in spray programmes.

If you do decide to grow for the shop, choose your crops carefully. Obviously, the crops must fit in with land capability, climate and the type of customer you serve. Give priority to:

* Crops that store well (potatoes and apples) or freeze well (sweetcorn, runner beans, raspberries) so that you attract customers who are looking for fresh, quality produce and who will make bulk purchases.

*   Crops that are easy to grow (rhubarb, asparagus, and Welsh onions are perennial crops that need minimal attention once established) or that fit easily into your existing production system. If you grow a large area of apples, put in a few unusual or old-fashioned varieties to add interest to the shop. If you already grow raspberries, add an assortment of hybrid berries for diversity, and add autumn fruiters to extend the season.

*   Crops that the supermarkets rarely handle (such as dessert gooseberries, Jerusalem artichokes, quinces, snap peas) or that you can present much better than even the best of the supermarkets i.e. spinach, soft fruit, cherries and plums.

Is it all worth it? By-passing the traditional links in the marketing chain certainly gives higher returns than normal market sales. It is difficult to give precise figures. Barker (1981), quoting from a survey at Reading University Farm Shop, states that *'the increased margins over normal available market returns varied from 19% for eggs to 32% for flowers, fruit and vegetables'*.

Table 12. Crop areas needed to supply 1,000 customers[1] for the period July, August, September

| Crop | Average consumption | | | | Crop data | | |
	per head per week (oz)[2]	per week (oz)	per week (lb)	per 13 wk period (lb)	yield/ acre (tonne)[3]	yield/ acre (lb)	area needed (acre)
		per 1,000 people					
Potatoes	36	36,000	2,250	29,250	14	31,360	0.93
Carrots	3.79	3,790	237	3,079	12	26,880	0.11
Cabbage	3.59	3,590	224	2,917	10	22,400	0.13
Onions	3.31	3,310	207	2,670	14	31,360	0.09
Peas	0.87	870	54	702	2	4,480	0.15
Cauliflowers	3.27	3,270	204	2,656	4,800 head at 2lb	9,600	0.28
Lettuce	2.59	2,590	162	2,104	18,000 head at 8oz	9,000	0.23
						Total	1.92

Notes:

1. Average 'customer sale' has been equated with average 'consumption per head per week'. This is based on the assumption that one customer shops for a family of 2-3 people, but that this effect is offset by a shopping frequency (in July-Sept) of 2-3 times weekly.

2. Data from National food survey for 1986 (see "Food Statistics", page 68).

3. Data from Nix (1987) Farm Management Pocketbook.

Hygiene

'Any person who handles the food must . . . refrain from spitting and the use of tobacco and snuff when handling or in a room with open food.' (Food Hygiene (General) Regulations 1970).

It is in the interest of any farmer with a farm shop to maintain the highest standards of hygiene and cleanliness. It is good common sense and good business sense. It is also a legal requirement.

The *Food Act 1984* and the amended *Food Hygiene (General) Regulations 1970* lay down standards for:

* Food hygiene.
* Food premises.
* Contents and labelling of food.
* Registration of premises selling food.

The Act empowers local authorities to make bye-laws relating to hygiene and food premises. It also provides for Health Authority inspection of premises, and for sampling and analysis of food.

The regulations are many and complex. They are particularly stringent for dairy products, meat, cooked foods and unpackaged (open) foods. They apply to farm shops and to associated premises such as food preparation areas, stores and toilets. Many of the regulations cover basic stipulations for cleanliness of premises and equipment. Others cover specific requirements such as the provision of handbasins with hot and cold water.

If you are planning to set up a farm shop it is sensible to discuss your plans with your local Health Inspector; it is better to initiate the contact than to go ahead and wait for the routine inspection. It is absolutely essential to do so if you hope to sell meat or ice cream, cook on the premises or butcher livestock.

Insurance

The addition of a farm shop to a farming enterprise is likely to require insurance over and above the normal farm policy. Be sure to inform your insurers of your retailing activities, and get advice on appropriate cover, particularly for the following:

* Contents of farm shop.

* Shop equipment.
* Public liability in case of claims arising out of accident or injury to customers or visitors to the farm. This is especially important if you have a farm trail, children's play area or visitor access to livestock.
* Employer's liability to cover personal injury to employees while at work.
* Product liability.
* Loss of money from the premises, on the way to the bank, or in the night safe of the bank.

Do not try to skimp on insurance for any of the above. Full coverage is essential. You may also want to cover for consequential loss e.g. for loss of income for some weeks as result of a farm shop fire.

The value of service contracts for equipment is arguable (see under Equipment—insurance).

Labelling

Good produce is worthy of good presentation and labelling. Labelling gives the customer information. It also creates an image. Labels of diverse colour, shape, size and script give a sloppy piecemeal impression. A uniform system of labelling suggests care and pride in the produce.

Sets of plastic labels allowing different combinations of product, price, grade and country of origin are available for fruit and vegetables. They are clear and practical and not unreasonable in price, but they leave little scope for adding supplementary information, they do not cover all farm shop products and they give a 'plastic' image associated with a supermarket rather than a farm shop. Handwritten cards make more work but are more personal and flexible. Cardboard is expensive to buy: try your printer for off-cuts.

Produce labels for prepacks or jars need careful thought. On a small scale the peel-off labels of the Able-Label type are cheap (£3.25 per thousand), look good, and will get you started. As soon as you know you are really in business get professional help with design, wording and legalities. An attractive label on a jar of jam can make all the difference between a utilitarian purchase and an exciting gift.

Food labelling regulations apply both to display labels for bulk produce and to labels on individual packs of food. Regulations pertaining to the labelling of fresh fruit and vegetables are set out in the EEC standards. Clear signs are required giving name of product, variety and grade (where applicable), place of origin (for imported produce) and price.

Regulations for manufactured products are more complex. Requirements cover lists of ingredients—including all additives; in some cases, information on durability ('best before' or 'sell-by' date); storage information (e.g. 'keep refrigerated once opened'); name and address of manufacturer or packer, and, in some cases, instructions for use.

The main requirements are set out in the *Food Labelling Regulations 1984*; other regulations are included in the *Trade Descriptions Act 1968* and in the *Weights and Measures* legislation. Regulations vary according to type of produce and whether or not it is pre-packed. Read the regulations pertaining to the goods you sell and, if in doubt, seek guidance.

If you make produce such as jams or pickles on a small scale, for sale in your own shop only, and if you comply with the spirit of the law, the authorities will tend to deal kindly with you if you err in detail. If you manufacture for sale to other outlets then your labelling *must* be correct in every minute way and it is worth paying for advice.

Layout of shop

Design the layout of your farm shop with the following in mind:
*   Efficient customer flow.
*   Efficient flow of goods.
*   Rural image.

Customer flow: Plan entrances and exits to assist in developing a 'traffic pattern'. Plan, the layout of counters and shelves so as to guide your customers naturally past each display area, finishing up at the check out area. (See also Display of goods.)

The aisles should be wide enough (minimum of four and a half feet wide) to avoid congestion, to cope with a push-chair and to take a trolley if you are handling bulky goods. Avoid a cramped check-out area—customers need space not only for packing up their purchases but

This shop has an entrance on the left, and is designed so that customers pass everything in the shop before reaching the checkout on the right and the exit door.

also for organizing children, prams, handbags, gloves . . .

Flow of goods: Do not underestimate the size of storage and working areas needed as back up to a shop; unpacking, re-packing, labelling and storage are best done outside the actual sales area. Make sure that messy jobs, temporary clutter and waste are kept behind the scenes.

Adequate storage areas are vital for stock rotation; cramped facilities waste time, cause muddles and are difficult to keep clean. Connecting doorways between storage area, work area and shop should be wide enough to take a trolley; make sure all floors are at the same level.

Keep in the shop only sufficient produce for topping up the fastest selling items; avoid cluttering the shop with half-empty boxes.

Rural image: Building layout must enable you to work efficiently, but try to preserve the rural image. If you are lucky enough to have the use of an old farm building in a rural setting make it work for you. Brick, stone, wood and basketwork enhance the image—leave the shiny plastic and the stainless steel to the supermarkets. Think twice before you rip out the inside of a building; maybe an old loose box, fitted with scatter cushions and toys, would make a haven for toddlers? Maybe a feed trough in the old cowshed could be turned into a display bin? Use your imagination to see if you can retain just a few farming features to distinguish your farm shop from the High Street shop or the supermarket.

Make sure you have adequate parking near the shop and safe access for children between shop and play area.

Leisure facilities

'Even if you are on the right tracks you will get run over if you just sit there.' Will Roger.

Department Stores in Japan pay a fortune for land yet they devote precious space to in-store leisure facilities. Planning authorities in the UK are also waking up to the benefits of adding recreational and educational facilities to their shopping malls. If, as seems likely, Sunday trading eventually becomes legal, the combination of shopping and leisure activities in the city centres will surely grow. Farmers selling fresh produce are permitted to open on Sundays, so can get a head start in developing combined shopping and leisure facilities.

Freshness of produce is likely to remain the foremost lure to draw the shopper to the farm but fun can come a close second. Increasing leisure brings ever-increasing opportunities for family outings to the countryside. A farm shop can satisfy the need for 'somewhere to go and something to do'.

Todays children are tomorrows customers. Keep them amused. An old tractor painted up is a marvellous attraction.

Some customers will drive to a farm just to buy a few pounds of Bramleys and Cox. More will be attracted if offered a wide selection of apples and pears, with tasters and with information about the characteristics and uses of the different varieties. Customers will come, and come again, if offered a play area for the children; a farm trail; farm tours; a chance to see, hear, smell and touch farm animals; fishing or sports facilities. Try to offer something different and special. The same applies to refreshments. Most people will stick to tea or coffee, but try adding further options. Maybe freshly pressed fruit juices or a spiced, mulled apple juice in winter? Put the emphasis on refreshments which make use of your own home-grown produce. Perhaps you could pass on some recipes or give occasional cookery demonstrations? The possibilities are as varied and wide as your imagination.

Make use of your family's enthusiasms and expertise. Do not be afraid to experiment—the more 'way out' and the more newsworthy the better. You need not invest a great deal of money. There is much to be said for starting up the leisure facilities in a modest way and adding something new each year; customers enjoy sharing in the growth.

Leisure facilities do not necessarily provide direct income but they do create a happy atmosphere which is intrinsically satisfying and a highly effective form of advertising.

Mark-up and margins

Definition of accounting terms is fraught with problems. Some terms, such as gross margin, are used quite differently in relation to farm management than in relation to retailing. The terms used in this publication are: *mark-up*, *margin on sales*, *trading margin* and *profit margin*.

Mark-up and margin on sales both concern the difference between the purchase price of goods (P) and the selling price of the goods (S). The mark-up relates this difference (S−P) back to the purchase price, whereas the margin on sales relates it to the selling price.

Mark-up on purchases: If you purchase goods for £100 and sell them for £120 you have added (marked-up) £20 on your purchase. The percentage mark up is:

$$\frac{(S-P)}{P} \times 100 = \frac{20}{100} \times 100 = 20\%$$

The mark-up is used to calculate the selling price of bought-in goods. A mark-up of 50% is commonly used for fruit and vegetables; this means that apples bought for 10p/lb will retail at 15p/lb. The mark-up is generally lower on groceries (15–30%) and higher on gifts (50–100% or more).

Margin on sales: If you buy grocery goods for £100 (P) and sell them for £120 (S) you have added a margin of £20; expressed as a percentage of sales this is:

$$\frac{(S-P)}{S} \times 100 = \frac{20}{120} \times 100 = 16.67\%$$

The margin on sales is important for interpreting financial results. Retail trade statistics give average margins as 18% for groceries, 24% for butchers, and 25% for greengrocers (see Retail Statistics).

Trading margin: If you buy for £100 (P) and sell for £120 (S) and have incurred running costs (R) of £10, your trading margin is:

$$S - (P + R) = 120 - (100 + 10) = £10.$$

The trading margin represents the return for capital inputs plus the reward to the shopkeeper and spouse for labour and management.

Profit margin: The profit margin is similar to the trading margin except that a capital charge has been included i.e. if you buy for £100, sell for £120 and incur running costs of £10 and capital charge (C) of £2 the profit margin is:

$$S - (P + R + C) = 120 - (100 + 10 + 2) = £8$$

The profit margin represents the reward to shopkeeper and spouse for their labour and management.

Table 13. Margins for a hypothetical greengrocer's shop

Sales (S)	£100,000/year
Purchases (P)	£ 75,000/year
Running costs (R)	£ 18,000/year
Capital costs (C)	£ 2,000/year
Sales – purchases (S–P)	£ 25,000 / year

$$\text{MARGIN ON SALES} \quad \frac{S-P}{S} \times 100 = \frac{25,000}{100,000} \times 100 = 25\%$$

$$\text{TRADING MARGIN} \quad \frac{S-(P+R)}{S} \times 100 = \frac{100,000-93,000}{100,000} \times 100 = 7\%$$

$$\text{PROFIT MARGIN} \quad \frac{S-(P+R+C)}{S} \times 100 = \frac{100,000-95,000}{100,000} \times 100 = 5\%$$

Table 13 shows the margins for a greengrocer's shop with sales averaging £2,000 per week. The figures indicate the order of magnitude of the margins for such a shop. Unfortunately there is insufficient published information to draw up reliable yardsticks either for setting targets or for evaluation of financial results for a farm shop.

The importance of calculating margins for a business lies in assessing year-to-year progress *within* the business. As the shop grows, margins should improve and eventually stabilise.

A low margin on sales suggests you need to examine wastage, buying, and pricing policy. A steady sales margin but low trading margin indicates high running costs. A steady trading margin but low profit margin indicates high capital inputs. Check that there is a good reason for a drop in margins or analyse results carefully and tighten management accordingly.

Money

'Money is just something to make book-keeping convenient'
H. L. Hunt, Texas Oil Billionnaire.

Handling large amounts of cash is not a normal farm activity. It feels rather like playing monopoly—money keeps changing hands but gives little sense of reality so it is easy to get careless about it. Work out standard procedures to ensure accuracy.

Till procedure: Start the day with a fixed amount of change in each till and a dated record sheet (see under Records). During the day:

* Keep the tills tidy—use the compartments to separate the money into different denominations; keep bank notes facing in the same direction (this saves subsequent reshuffling to get the money ready for the bank).

* Avoid overflowing tills. Transfer surplus cash to safe or bank at regular intervals.

* Keep records of all payments, receipts and errors on the record sheet as you go along. It does not matter what mistakes you make on the till so long as you put an explanatory note in the till immediately.

* Keep an eye on the till rolls—most have a warning red stripe on the paper to tell you that they are

running low. Operating the tills without till paper is a disaster both for the till and for the accounts.
* Encourage customers to take the receipt slip so that they have the account with them in case of error.

End of day:
* Get a till read-out and clear the till for the next day. The read-out shows the total takings, analysis of takings, customer numbers and cash paid out. Clip the read-out to the daily record sheet together with invoices for any payments made from the till.
* Clear cash from till (leave tills open at night to save them from being smashed open in case of burglary). Remove the next day's change to the safe; remove the rest of the takings to the safe or bank.
* Write up the accounts on a daily basis. Muddles are far easier to sort out while the events of the day are still fresh in the memory.

Neighbours, compete or co-operate?

Competition can come from different sources, principally: local village shops; out of town supermarkets and hyper-markets; other farm shops.

Local village shops: In some cases where local shop and post office have been hit by dwindling populations, a farm shop may be able to save the situation by combining basic services for the locals with speciality goods for customers drawn from nearby towns. The RDC is likely to be part-icularly helpful in such cases (see Appendix 2). Beware of duplicating the activities of a good village shop in your vicinity lest you both go under.

Out of town supermarkets: Do not underestimate the economy of scale and the one-stop-shopping advantages of the larger multiples. People may profess to dislike such impersonal shopping but they will use it regardless—especial-ly in bad weather.

Other farmers: PYO farms and farm shops are proliferating; the introduction of Diversification Grants in 1988 is likely to add to the pressure. In some areas competition between neighbouring PYO farms has led to a fierce price war. Be-fore contemplating setting up a new PYO unit or farm shop look carefully at the local competition to make sure you are not encroaching on a saturated market.

If you are already established and someone else starts up 'on your patch' try to fight on the basis of high quality of goods and high standards of service to your customers rather than on slashed prices. One grower summed it up like this: *'Clearly we cannot charge 70p/lb for PYO raspberries when our competitors are on 30p! But we can with some justification charge 42p. Our customers are quite ready to pay a little more for top quality produce, together with better staff, better advice, better layout and facilities than the grower who opens his gates only to clear up the scraps after the crop has been picked for the market. We have also learned not to panic. If a competitor is advertising fruit at a silly price there is probably a reason for it—the low price may be the only good thing about it'.*

If your farm shop and a neighbour's farm shop sell essentially different produce, if you both maintain high standards, and if you are able to co-operate, you are onto a potential winner. Try to work together on advertising, signposting and promotions. If possible, plan your range of goods, services and opening times to complement each other's activities. Get your locality known as 'the area for a farm-fresh outing' and enjoy the benefit of each other's customers.

This may sound like a counsel of perfection but it can and does happen. There are other examples of co-operation in the 'farm-fresh' scene. PYO growers in some counties regularly co-operate for generic advertising, in particular to alert the public to the start of the strawberry season and to encourage customers to get out to their nearest fruit farm. Co-operation allows effective advertising on a scale which no individual farmer could afford.

Growers with farm shops can benefit from an exchange of produce. A grower famed for his Comice pears has a regular link with a grower of quality Cox apples some 30 miles away. Each season a load or two of fruit is exchanged. No money changes hands, but both farm shops benefit from an extended range of top quality produce.

Officialdom

'If all the regulations and statutory requirements which are available to control farm sales of various kinds were enforced, most operators would be obliged to cease trading.' Grower Books (1979).

Direct retailing from the farm brings the farmer into contact with a tangle of regulations and statutory requirements. Legislation aims to safeguard health, safety, fair trading, consumer rights, landscape and environment. Most of the requirements seem sensible; a few seem inordinately pedantic. Most are rigorously applied; a few are conveniently overlooked.

Attitudes towards regulations vary. It is worth recognising the wisdom underlying the legislation and attempting to comply with it. Find out about the regulations before you set up shop or while sales are still on a pin-money basis. Once you are sure that you want to expand into a serious business ask for official guidance. Most authorities will go out of their way to be helpful if asked for advice while you are still at the planning stage.

An excellent guide to the legal requirements has recently been published (NFU, 1987). To avoid duplication, only brief indications of the major regulations are given here. They are included in the following sections:

Building control	Planning permission
Consumer rights and protection	Rates
Food hygiene	Signposts
Insurance	Value Added Tax
Labelling	Weights and measures

Opening times

You can make your own rules about farm shop opening times but some points are worth watching:

*   Consistency. Once you have settled on the times and publicised them, stick to them. If you advertise the shop as 'Open 9–6 daily' then the shop must be manned during those hours, come hurricane, haytime or headache. If, however, you state 'Open 9 a.m. to 5 p.m. or to dusk in *fine* weather' you can' spend a wet evening with a good book and a clear conscience.

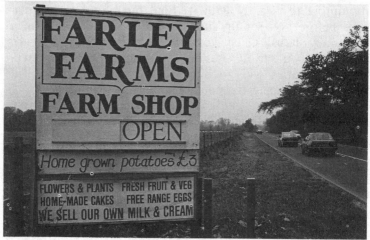

Consistent opening hours are a help to the customer (top). A sliding CLOSED/OPEN sign can spare customers the frustration of driving up a farm road to find the shop closed (bottom).

* Keep the hours low initially and increase them as trade warrants. Customers welcome increased trading hours but curtailment is bitterly resented.

* Simple and *regular* hours are best. '9 a.m. to 5 p.m. daily' is easily remembered and easy to advertise. If seasonality dictates frequent changes in opening times encourage customers to telephone before they drive out to the farm.

Season of opening: Retailing milk, meat or eggs entails all year round opening. Opening times for fruit, vegetables and bedding plants are dictated largely by their season. The comings and goings of customers will dictate opening times if you cater for campers or passing tourist trade.

Shops based on sales of fresh home-grown seasonal produce have three options:

* Open the shop only as and when your produce is available. This is possible if you are on a main road with a lot of passing traffic and your signposting is good. In remote areas you will find it difficult to attract enough customers.

* Open the shop throughout the harvest season, say from the first of the rhubarb in spring through to the last of the blackberries in the autumn. This will mean growing crops specifically for the farm shop in order to avoid lean periods when you have very little to sell. Continuity of supply facilitates running the shop and holding the customers. However, it demands complex growing skills and brings the danger of producing a wide range of mediocre quality crops (see Growing fruit and vegetables for the shop).

* Keep the shop open right through the year by adding bought-in produce. (See under Buying-in.)

Customer numbers and expenditure vary widely through the year—the pattern depends on type of produce, location and weather. For greengrocers, summer weather prompts more frequent shopping with lower expenditure per visit. Holiday time decimates trade in the cities and transfers it to the tourist areas. Autumn is unloved in the greengrocery trade (due to a combination of low prices and surplus produce in home gardens). Christmas sales rise to a dramatic peak followed by a long, low trough. For farm shops the classic picture is blurred by the seasonal draw of home-grown produce and by the attraction of a run out to the country on a fine day.

Days of opening: Factors to take into account in deciding how many days a week to open include: perishability of goods; availability and cost of labour; your own needs; pattern of trade; leisure facilities on the farm.

Perishability of goods: If a high proportion of your income is derived from the sale of strawberries which ripen over a three week period then it makes sense to open every daylight hour of every precious day during that short period. If you sell milk and cream or summer salad crops you will need to be open at least six days a week. Green-grocery sales can be run on a four or five-day a week basis during the cooler months. At the other extreme, it may be more economic to restrict the opening of a small gift shop to weekends and holidays only.

Labour: It costs little more than £20 to staff a shop for an extra day; this sum can be recouped by the sale of:

* 33 lb PYO raspberries at 60p/lb (assuming that the fruit would go to waste if the farm were closed for the day).

* 200 lb apples at 26p/lb (retail value £52; assuming that the apples would be sold wholesale at 16p/lb if the shop were closed).

* £71 worth of bought-in goods (assuming a mark-up of 28%).

You need to consider the availability and the flexibility of labour. Can you make use of farm shop staff for any other work if the weather is wet and customers are scant? Can you cope with a sudden rush if the weather is fine?

Your own needs: Running a retail outlet makes pressing demands on time and energy. Get your priorities right and arrange opening days to give yourself a break, at least in the slack season.

Patterns of trade: Bread, milk and cheaper cuts of meat sell steadily throughout the week. Gifts, flowers and bedding plants, and the more expensive cuts of meat sell best at weekends. Plan your opening days accordingly.

Leisure facilities: Open the shop to tie in with leisure facilities on the farm. Sunday sales of perishable goods such as fresh fruit, vegetables and freshly-cooked produce are permitted under the *Shops Act 1950*. (There are strange anomalies in the law; for instance, the Sunday sale of home produced eggs is permitted from temporary stalls but not from a permanent farm shop.) Check with your local authority to see whether there are any local bye-laws concerning Sunday trading.

Figure 13 shows daily customer flow at Mortimer Hill Farm Shop during the last week of term-time and the first week of the school holidays. The figures relate to combined

Figure 13. Distribution of customers throughout the week

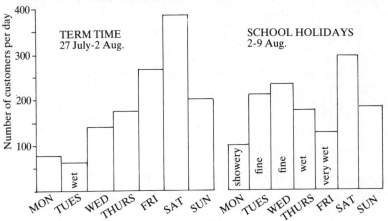

Source: Mortimer Hill Farm Shop 1987
Note: Data refer to farm shop plus PYO, but the latter is of only minor importance by the end of July.

farm shop and PYO trade, but the latter is only a minor factor at the end of July (strawberries and the main varieties of raspberries are already finished). The figure illustrates clearly the normal term-time shopping pattern with a build up of trade towards the Saturday peak. The school holiday pattern shows a wider spread of activity through the week— the farm shop is as much a place to take children for an outing as a place to stock up; daily fluctuations are due to weather rather than any classic pattern of shopping.

Hours of opening: It is silly to sit in an empty shop waiting for customers and it is equally silly to greet potential customers with a 'closed' sign. Study the pattern of traffic flow in the area around your farm:

*   When does the commuter traffic pass?
*   Is there a pattern of shopping linked to the school traffic?
*   Is there a demand for lunchtime shopping?
*   Is there any passing tourist trade?
*   Do nearby market days or early closing days affect the traffic?
*   Can you discern a pattern of trade in competing retail outlets?

It may be wise to start with restricted hours and get feedback from your customers as to their shopping habits and requirements.

Figure 14. Distribution of customers throughout the day

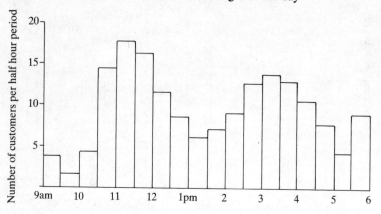

Source: Mortimer Hill Farm Shop 1987
Note: Figures relate to the farm shop only on a typical fine Friday in October

Figure 14 shows the pattern of customer flow at Mortimer Hill Farm Shop on a typical Friday on a fine day in October. The day starts with a handful of shoppers on their way to work, then a quiet period until the build up to peak activity in mid-morning. Slow mid-day trade is followed by the OAPs and pram-pushers in the early afternoon, followed by the busy afternoon period associated with the school run. A final spurt of commuter shopping ends the day.

Such patterns change in the school holidays, and are also affected by the weather. Nevertheless, they are a guide for essential opening times and staffing requirements.

Organically grown produce

'In the long run, the organic movement needs to reach out and attract the average shopper and not to be restricted to a small elite who will put up with anything.' Blake, 1987.

One of the few bright spots in the farming world, with a real and expanding demand for produce, is the market for organically grown and 'additive-free' foods. Food and health issues are no longer the sole domain of cranks and food faddists. There is widespread concern about chemical additives and residues in food. In an opinion poll of consumers commissioned by the NFU (Grower, 1988), over half the adults questioned said they would be interested in buying organically-grown produce, and 37% said they would be willing to pay a premium for such produce.

The change from conventional farming to organic production is difficult, especially in intensive horticulture. Do not underestimate the technical difficulties. Labour requirements for weed control are necessarily high, pests and diseases may cause loss of yield and quality as compared with conventionally grown produce. Advice is now available through an organic advisory service (see Appendix 2), and ADAS is slowly being drawn in, but there are still considerable gaps in knowledge and experience. If you are considering a change to organic production methods contact the appropriate Association for information (addresses in Appendix 2).

The organic movement in the UK has been dogged by three major problems:
* Multiplicity of standards.
* Lack of government-sponsored research and development.
* Lack of cohesive marketing structure.
The lack of marketing structure can actually work to the advantage of the small grower able to sell produce direct to the customer from the farm shop. It does however confront the farm shop with the problem of meeting customers' continuing demand for fresh organic produce once the growing season is over. *'We always found that our regular clientele in our farmshop were in direct proportion to the range and continuity of supply of our produce'* (Blake, 1987).

Buying-in organically-grown produce presents real problems, both in continuity of supply and in quality. Marketing organisations *are* evolving but the network of suppliers is still incomplete. Much of the produce is imported and supplies are erratic. *'At least 60% of supermarket sales of organically-grown produce was imported last year. The figure could be as high as 75%'* (Wendover, 1987). The imported produce comes mainly from Holland, Germany and Israel.

Our own experience handling organically-grown produce confirms that the demand exists but that it is

difficult to meet it. (See under Mortimer Hill, a case study).
We were reluctant to disappoint the enthusiastic and caring
clientele but even more reluctant to lower our standards.

Packaging

An estimated one per cent of turnover spent on packaging
(Thompson, 1988) means an expenditure of £1000 per year
for the 'average' shop with a turnover of £100,000 per year.
Some farm shops opt for the cheapest possible packaging—
'let the goods speak for themselves, the wrappings get
chucked out'. Other farm shops use high quality carrier
bags with the name of the farm printed on them—'the
publicity justifies the expense'. Take your pick!

There is a wealth of choice of packaging materials.
Ask one or two local packaging suppliers (look under
Packaging Materials in the Yellow Pages) for a catalogue.
There are surprising price differences; white paper bags
are about 15% dearer than brown paper bags, and polythene
bags cost more than twice as much as the high-density
plastic bags. Once you know what you want, compare prices
from different sources and try to get a bulk discount.

*Attractive gift packaging can spread your name and reputation to
recipients.*

Gift packs: The humblest of produce can be converted into a prime gift if the quality and presentation are right. Have a few gift packs at the ready, and maybe provide straw-lined gift-baskets which customers can fill with a selection of goods of their own choice. Do not skimp on good quality gift paper and always add a label with the name and address of your farm. Readiness to make up a gift package is a service much appreciated by customers, and it spreads your name and fame to the recipient.

Pick-your-own

'The appeal of the PYO field in the early days was part novelty, part value for money, part fun. We ought to have known that it would take more than cheap strawberries to keep the public coming. Two bad summers have rammed the point home.' Editorial in the Grower, 7th April, 1988.

Many farm shops have grown from an initial PYO enter-prise. A survey of 419 PYO farms showed that nearly half already ran a farm shop with *'many more intending to open one'* (Grower, 1988). It is a logical extension. With customers already on the farm it simply means adding on a wider range of goods and services.

Addition of farm shop to PYO enterprise: Suppose you already have a PYO unit on the farm. Is it worth adding a farm shop? Yes if:

*   There is a demand for ready-picked produce. Some customers enjoy picking their own produce, others lack time, energy or enthusiasm and are prepared to pay more for picked produce.
*   There is a demand for complementary products such as cream for the PYO strawberries.
*   There are seasonal gaps in the supply of home pro-duce which can be spanned with good quality pro-duce bought from a neighbouring grower.
*   You detect an obvious shopping gap in your area or a demand for 'one stop shopping'. This can be re-searched by talking to your PYO customers and care-ful investigation of shopping facilities in the neigh-bourhood.
*   You have under-utilised labour and spare buildings on the farm; also if you are contemplating the add-ition of leisure facilities.

Addition of PYO to a farm shop: Suppose you already have a specialist farm shop selling eggs, or meat or gifts. Is it worth adding a PYO fruit and vegetable unit? Yes if:

* You already have a good flow of customers to the farm, and it is easy to expand sales facilities to cover the PYO produce.

* You have suitable land for PYO adjacent to the farm shop. (People hate to walk, and internal transport to and from the crops is expensive.)

* Soil, facilities and know-how are suitable for growing a diversity of crops.

* There is sufficient labour at the ready to cope with the sudden seasonal demands of the PYO and yet keep the farm and the shop running smoothly.

* You accept that the PYO will cause some damage to crops. Either allocate a specific area to the PYO, or come to terms with the fact that unsystematic picking by customers will make professional harvesting (for shop or market) more difficult.

Planning and costings: Costings for the major PYO crops and technical advice (suitable varieties, layout, spacing for PYO) are available from ADAS. It is well worth taking advice; PYO is much better documented than the 'grey area' of farm shops.

Planning permission

Town and Country planning, administered through the local Planning Authority, is concerned with regional structure and development. The regulations are set out in: *Town and Country Planning Act 1971*; *Town and Country Planning General Development Orders, 1977–1985*; *Town and Country Planning (Agricultural and Forestry Development in National Parks etc.,) Special Development Order 1986*. A summary of the legislation is given in the *NFU Legal Guide* (NFU 1987).

The *Planning Act of 1971* makes it necessary to obtain planning permission for:

* Building or engineering works (except for purely agricultural purposes).

* Change of use of land or buildings (except for purely agricultural purposes).

This sounds simple, but it is not. The agricultural exemptions apply only to exclusive agricultural use and even then there are stipulations limiting the maximum permissible size and height of buildings and their proximity to a highway.

Planning permission is *not* required for converting an existing farm building into a farm shop for the sale of fresh, home-grown produce only. Permission *is* required if the shop is to sell produce, even home-grown produce, that is 'substantially altered or adapted'. Washed carrots would probably pass as 'unaltered' but cooked beetroot or frozen raspberries would probably be deemed to have been 'altered'.

Similarly, planning permission is probably needed if sales are to include jointed meat, dressed oven-ready poultry, fruit juices or preserves. It is definitely needed if the shop is to sell pasteurised milk, butter, cheese or bought-in produce.

If you think your enterprise is likely to require planning permission consult your local planning authority at an early stage. The local planning authority will request advice from the highway authority on any application for planning permission for a farm shop. Where access is from a trunk road the highway authority has the power to refuse the granting of planning permission. You should therefore liaise with the highway authority if access or increased traffic flow are likely to be a problem.

It is far better to seek advice and follow requirements than to go ahead and risk being confronted with an enforcement notice stopping your activity. Present policies aim to encourage farm diversification, create rural employment and make use of redundant farm buildings. In this climate the regulations may well be eased. They should not be ignored.

Pricing

'The mechanics of running a business are really not very complicated when you get down to essentials. You have to make (or grow or buy) some stuff and sell it to somebody else for more than it cost you. That's about all there is to it except for a few million details.' John L. McCaffrey, former President of International Harvester.

Setting price levels is one of the most crucial—and most difficult—issues in retailing. Are you aiming to provide the best possible value for your customers consistent with covering expenses and making a modest profit? Or do you subscribe to the go-grab philosophy of 'charge as much as the market will stand?' In practice, farm shop retailing is more likely to revolve around questions of survival than of philosophy.

A few rules of thumb can be applied to determine a broad pricing policy. Finer tuning depends on 'finger-tip feeling'; herein lies the fun and the art of retailing.

Pricing policy—broad principles: The prices you charge for goods can be set with reference to:

* Cost of production.
* Wholesale prices (obtainable from NFU Market Intelligence, Radio Market Reports, Prestel, the press, or direct from market sources).
* Retail prices (readily ascertained from shops in your locality or from the media).
* A combination of the above.

In a study of farmers undertaking direct marketing Barker (1981) found that 40% used a combination of criteria, 26% based their shops prices on wholesale prices and 19% based them on retail prices (see Table 14). The decision depends largely on the type of product sold and whether ready-picked, PYO or bought-in.

Pricing fruit and vegetables: The price charged for PYO fruit and vegetables is generally set between the wholesale and retail price. For strawberries (high wastage and high consumption in the field) price tends to be pitched nearer the retail level; for rhubarb (unpalatable raw!) the price tends to be nearer the wholesale level. The price of ready-picked farm produce is also set between the wholesale and retail levels, varying with quantity and quality of produce grown, perishability and demand.

The retail price of bought-in fruit and vegetables is based on wholesale price plus mark-up (in the region of 40% to 60%) depending on whether the produce is bought from a local grower, wholesale market or secondary whole-saler, and whether or not the price paid includes the cost of delivery.

Pricing of plants and nursery stock: The selling price of bedding plants and nursery stock can be linked either to wholesale prices (available from growers' catalogues or from market sources) or to local retail prices. Special-

Table 14. Methods of pricing used by farmers undertaking direct marketing in 1978

Pricing policy	Number of Respondents
Refer to local wholesale prices	26
Keep in line with shop prices	19
Set the price for each product in relation to its current supply and demand	5
Add a margin to the cost of production	6
Some combination of the above	43
	(n = 116)

Source: Barker (1981)

ities and rarities demand a higher mark-up than standard goods, commensurate with the marketing risk involved.

Pricing food products: The selling price of processed foods and food products depends on whether they are home-made or bought in. Prices for home produce are most readily calculated on a 'cost plus' basis (include the cost of labour, services, packaging and labelling, as well as the cost of ingredients) with allowance for rarity value and for know-how.

Bought-in products sell at wholesale price plus mark-up. Some manufacturers and wholesalers give a recommended retail price (RRP) in their catalogues—a great boon. It is also worth keeping an eye on local retail prices and making adjustments if there is a wide discrepancy.

Pricing gifts and craft goods: Books are a joy to handle as they come marked with the retail price (they are invoiced to the retailer at selling price less discount of 30%–33%).

Gifts and craft goods are the most difficult to price. Margins are high and you need to become familiar with the price structure for similar goods in your own area. Pricing of home-crafted goods is probably the most difficult of all; cost of production, demand, prices of similar products have to be taken into account. Allowance has to be made for the input of skill as well as labour and for uniqueness of product. Seek advice and resist the temptation to under-value your goods to get them selling.

Farm shop image: You may want to adjust all prices in relation to the 'image' of your shop. You cannot be the cheapest if you aim to provide a personal service; it takes time to make people welcome, to advise on produce, to deal with individual requests for goods that you do not normally stock.

If quality, friendliness, location and opening hours add up to give a unique service then your prices will have to reflect this. If, on the other hand, your sole aim is to get customers into the shop, out again and off the farm with the utmost speed you will have to compete on price. Set clear aims as to image and pricing policy.

The finer tuning: The finer tuning of prices for individual items is an endless process. It consists of many small decisions which are of cumulative importance. Examples of the sort of considerations which affect pricing of individual greengrocery items are listed below. It is a random selection given only to illustrate the complexities:

* Perishability of goods. Two strategies are possible for highly perishable produce. Either take a high mark-up to compensate for the inevitable wastage. Or, take a very low mark-up in the hope of selling the produce fast.
* Surplus goods. If you have grown or bought too much of any one crop consider offering a 'Best Buy' at a reduced rate.
* Evening-out prices. The wholesale price of some goods (e.g. mushrooms) goes up and down like a yo-yo. It makes sense to fix a retail price and to stick to it regardless of fluctuations.
* Averaging out prices. Ten different varieties of apple at ten different prices causes confusion. Consider selling them all at the same price so that customers can 'mix and match' and try out new varieties.
* Consumer resistance. If produce is temporarily scarce and prices soar be prepared to take a lower mark-up until prices settle.
* Snob appeal. If you handle expensive luxury goods do not lose your nerve and offer them at give away prices. It can happen that exotic goods will not sell on a cheap ticket but are quickly taken up if well displayed and offered at a high price!

Price differentials: Give the customer as much information as possible to help make an informed choice. If you offer

English Tomatoes at 95p/lb and Canary Island Tomatoes at 45p/lb make sure that the boxes are close to each other so that quality can be compared. Label the 95p tomatoes clearly, pointing out that they are locally grown and the first of the season.

Similarly, if you have a good line in pet foods do not simply label it 'Good value 25p/tin'. Put the new brand alongside a well-known brand selling at 35p/tin and let the customers make their choice. People tend not to remember prices but they do notice price differentials.

Public relations

'He who whispers down a well about the goods he has to sell will not earn as many dollars as he who climbs a tree and hollers.'

A farm shop commits you to working with people. Lots of people. Many different sorts of people. Fine summer days will turn your farm into the focal point for a free outing. Are you prepared to cope with pram pushers congregating around the animals, OAPs clustering in the sunshine, the village bore ambushing you in order to tell you how to farm, youngsters screaming round the yard? If you are, you will soon be asked to cope also with group visits from kindergardens, schools, disabled and blind groups, Vietnamese refugees, horticultural societies, womens' guilds . . . it is endless. It is no way to make a fortune but it obviously fills a social need. And it does enlarge the clientele.

Some activities give a direct return in the form of free publicity in the local press. If the reporter from your local paper does not get drawn into your activities try writing your own Press Release and sending it to the Editor. Do not hesitate to blow your own trumpet—if interesting things are happening on your farm the readers will want to know. The opening of a farm trail, blossom time, shearing or spinning demonstrations, apple tastings—all are newsworthy and if you can add photographs so much the better. Photos of children and animals add instant appeal; conservation is news. You do not have to be a literary genius, all you need is an eye and an ear for the newsworthy, the editor will knock it into shape. A press release should be brief (never more than one side of A4 paper) but should be long enough to allow the editor to select the bits that interest him; add your name and telephone number so you can be contacted for further information.

Rates

A farm is exempt from rates. A shop is rated. What about a farm shop?

It is commonly believed that a farm shop selling only home-grown produce is exempt but that a farm shop selling bought-in produce is rated. In practice it is not so simple. There are several problems:

Definition of home-grown: Can 'home-grown' be applied to produce grown on a different part of the same farm or on a separate farm under the same ownership? Is a container plant 'home-grown' if it was bought in small and merely grown-on? Must it be grown-on for a week, a month or a year to qualify as 'home-grown'?

Definition of a shop: A purpose built shop used exclusively as a farm shop is likely to be considered rateable. Rates of between £4–£8 per square metre are commonly applied to the shop and associated areas such as food stores.

Can sales from a working area of the farm e.g. from a corner of the packing shed, be classed as farm shop sales? Calculation of rates is even more difficult in such cases.

Application of the regulations: Local Authorities vary in their interpretation of the regulations *(General Rate Act 1967)*. The NFU is aware of the problems and test cases on appeal to the Land Tribunal may clear some of the grey areas. Meanwhile the broad view of the NFU is that *'. . . farm shops are likely to be considered rateable since, in the view of the Inland Revenue, they constitute a separate commercial undertaking. This is true in a great many cases where farm shops, even if only selling the produce of the holding on which they stand, maintain separate accounts and have, in effect, exclusive use of either a building or an identifiable part of a building . . . It is open to argument whether any farm shop, on whatever scale, which sells only its own produce should be exempt from rates. Although the advice that the NFU has obtained suggests that this might be a difficult argument to sustain in some cases, it is clear that there are a great many smaller shops* *which should have a good chance of avoiding rates'* (NFU 1987).

Local experience suggests that attitudes are hardening as regards rating of farm shops. The small farm shop just starting up may escape rates for a year or two but growth and success will inevitably make the enterprise rateable. The axiom 'If it is worth doing it is probably rateable' seems to be the order of the day.

The NFU Legal Guide also points out that areas such as car parks may be liable to rates. This applies even where the car park is grassland, since the agricultural land exemption requires the land to be used only as meadow or pasture ground; use as a car park, even for part of the year, may render it liable for rates.

Records

A farm shop creates a continuous stream of bookwork. Keep up with it—or risk drowning.

Till records: Keep a record sheet in each till (Figure 15). Keep the forms simple but make sure that they are carefully filled in; errors, debts and payments must be recorded as they occur. At the end of each day staple together the record sheet, read-out for each till, and any relevant invoices.

Daily records: For each till, reconcile cash in till with till read-out. Note any discrepancies. Keep a day book listing:

*   Total takings (cash and cheques).
*   Analysis of sales.
*   Number of customers.
*   Payments into or from till (e.g. debts repaid, goods and wages paid out from the till).

Note major factors affecting the day's trade e.g. weather, start of school holidays.

Weekly records: Keep a record of total takings, total customer numbers and average expenditure per customer. Keep a record also of cash payments from the till, cash to float, and cash to the bank.

Monthly records: Add up the weekly totals, analyse payments, calculate monthly bank balance and check against bank statements, making allowances for outstanding transactions and, if necessary, for changes in stock.

The monthly figures for total turnover, customer numbers, customer expenditure, and margin on sales

(sales—purchases) are vital clues to understanding a business and pinpointing its problems. If takings are lower than anticipated is this due to lack of customers, low expenditure per customer or low margins? If the margin on sales is lower than anticipated is this due to low mark-up, poor purchasing or excessive wastage?

Annual records: Graphs of average weekly takings, customer numbers and expenditure per customer highlight progress and problems over the years. Look carefully also at changes in sales margin, trading margin and profit margin (see under Mark-up and margins) to see how expenditure changes in relation to level of takings.

Time spent keeping and interpreting records is time well spent. Records are the pulse of the business and essential for assessing progress and for decision making.

Figure 15. Till Record Sheet

Till No.	*Date* . . . .
Operator	*Hours*
. . . .	*to* . . . .
. . . .	*to* . . . .
. . . .	*to* . . . .
Paid from till	*sum*
. . . .	. . . .
. . . .	. . . .
. . . .	. . . .
Notes (errors etc)	
. . . .	. . . .

Note: This size of notebook fits into a till compartment. It is necessarily small, but the only logical and foolproof place to keep the till record sheets.

Retail statistics

Before you get excited at the vision of a thriving shop on your farm get the retail trade into perspective by taking a hard look at the retail statistics.

The Department of Trade and Industry carries out a statistical analysis of the retail trade every two years. The enquiry includes information from dairymen, butchers and poulterers, greengrocers and fruiterers, and grocers. Unfortunately there is no category relating specifically to farm shops.

Table 15 shows the number of retail businesses in Great Britain, and their turnover. It shows that while total turnover continues to increase over the years, the number of retail outlets continues to decline. The average size of shop is increasing. Be warned: if you are planning to set up a small, independent retail outlet you will be swimming against the tide.

Table 16 relates more specifically to the food trade. The proportion of total turnover taken by the large multiple retailers continues to grow; it reached 70% in 1984.

Tables 17 and 18 compare retail statistics for shops handling different types of food. Turnover per retail outlet in 1984 averaged about £75,000, £128,000 and £110,000 for greengrocers, butchers and the smaller grocers respectively, with margin on sales (sales−purchases) of about 25%, 24% and 18% respectively.

The ratio of capital investments to sales (see Table 18) was remarkably similar for greengrocers, butchers and the smaller grocers; all had annual capital inputs of about 1.6% of turnover. By contrast, the large grocers spent almost twice as much on capital inputs.

The final column in Table 18 (A−B) shows sales less purchases and capital inputs; this represents the proportion of turnover allocated to running costs plus profits. In the case of the average greengrocer this figure was 23.7%. Assuming that running costs accounted for 18%, then 5.7% of turnover (£4304) would have been left to cover the reward to the shopkeeper.

Table 15. Number of retail businesses and turnover, 1980, 1982, 1984

Year	Number of retail outlets	Turnover (£m)
1980	362,494	59,455
1982	349,659	69,784
1984	343,153	82,342

Table 16. Food retailers : form of organization and proportion of total turnover

	1982		1984	
Type of outlet	Number of outlets	% of total turnover	Number of outlets	% of total turnover
Single outlet retailer	73,890	23%	69,471	22%
Small multiple retailer	22,252	10%	19,985	8%
Large multiple retailer	18,632	67%	17,387	70%

Table 17. Retail Statistics by kind of business, totals 1984

	Number of businesses	Number of outlets	Total retail sales[1] (£m)	Margin on sales[2] (£m)	Capital expenditure[3] (£m)
Large grocery	100	9,997	20,436	3,708	630
Smaller grocery	32,130	35,921	3,966	681	62
Butcher	15,573	21,224	2,710	655	42
Greengrocer	13,711	16,527	1,248	314	20

1. Including VAT.
2. Sales less purchases. Figures exclude VAT and are adjusted for stock changes.
3. Cost of new building work plus the difference between acquisitions and disposals of capital inputs such as vehicles and equipment.
4. Larger retailer denotes a retail turnover of more than £10m in 1984.

Table 18. Data for 'average' businesses 1984

	Average sales per outlet (£)	A Margin on sales (%)	B Capital expenditure as % of sales	A–B[1]
Large grocery	2,044,213	19.1	3.1	16.0
Smaller grocery	110,408	17.8	1.6	16.2
Butcher	127,685	24.2	1.6	22.6
Greengrocer	75,512	25.3	1.6	23.7

1.   *This figure represents the proportion of total sales to cover running costs and return to shopkeeper and spouse for labour, management skills and profit.*

Source: Statistics in Tables 15–18 relate to Great Britain and are taken or derived from the Retailing Enquiry 1984, reported in 'British Business', 11th July, 1986, and in 'Business Monitor SDO25(1986)'. Enquiries take place every other year. Results for the 1986 enquiry are due to be published late 1988.

Rubbish

The disposal of rubbish is a wonderful example of escalating costs between a pin-money enterprise and a farm shop. Disposal of rubbish from a pin-money enterprise is easy; burn the burnable, compost the compostable and stuff the rest into your domestic dustbin. No further worry or expense.

Scaling up brings embarrassing mounds of rubbish which make demands on facilities and time. Burnable rubbish requires a proper incinerator near the shop or regular transport to a burning site; organic refuse must be removed well away from the shop to avoid fly and rat problems; the disposal of other rubbish requires a proper farm dump or payment for disposal by your local council.

Disposal of rubbish is vital for looks and hygiene. Aim at a layout which makes it easier to dispose of the rubbish in the right place than to 'sling it elsewhere for the time being'! Facilities should be conveniently close to the working area yet well out of sight of customers.

Rodents on a farm readily catch on to the delights of a varied diet obligingly concentrated in one building; routine control measures are essential. The pest control firms will undertake routine control for you—but at a price. If you do it yourself keep a constant watch for signs of activity and be ready for action. There is no easier way to lose customers than to allow them to come face to face with a rat!

Running costs

There is a dearth of data on farm shop running costs. This is not surprising in view of the difficulty of defining a farm shop and the varied size and nature of farm shops.

The family-run shop: Running costs for the smaller family-manned shop can be kept to a minimum with main expenditure likely to be on packaging, office expenses and advertising. If the shop is situated in or near the farm house, the family labour can be used with maximum efficiency—time is spent in the shop only as and when necessary without travelling time and 'captive time'. A shop that would not be economic if it had to be specially manned can be a very useful addition to the farm income under these conditions.

The larger shop: Once a farm shop outgrows its 'mainly family-worked' size, the major running expense is labour. Accounting practice excludes family labour as a running cost, so accounts for the family-worked shop look quite different from those of the larger shop.

A shop can be very labour efficient if worked by just one person who is able to tackle the ordering, display, cleaning and bookwork in between serving customers. As the shop grows and more labour is employed, the slack periods between customers are not always so well utilised. After considerable further growth, tasks can be delegated more easily and labour use again becomes more efficient.

If labour accounts for about 10% of shop takings (greengrocery goods) the other running costs total about 8% (see Figure 16). Advertising may well be the next biggest expense followed by packaging, repairs and renewals and transport. An example of the order of magnitude is suggested in Figure 17.

Figure 16. Purchases and running costs as a proportion of turnover

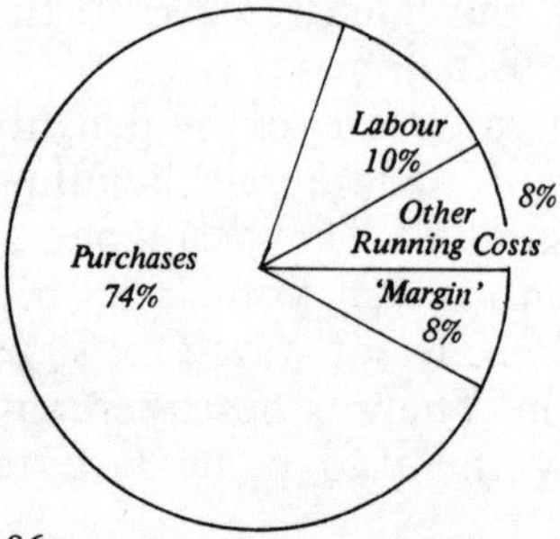

Labour 10%
Other Running Costs
'Margin' 8%
8%
Purchases 74%

Figure 17. Distribution of farmshop running costs

Packaging 5.6%
Repairs 5.6%
Transport 5.6%
Advertising 7.2%
Bank & Accountant 3.9%
Heat & Light 3.3%
Rates 3.3%
Tel/Office 2.7%
Insurance 1.7%
Depreciation & Misc 5.6%
Labour 55.5%

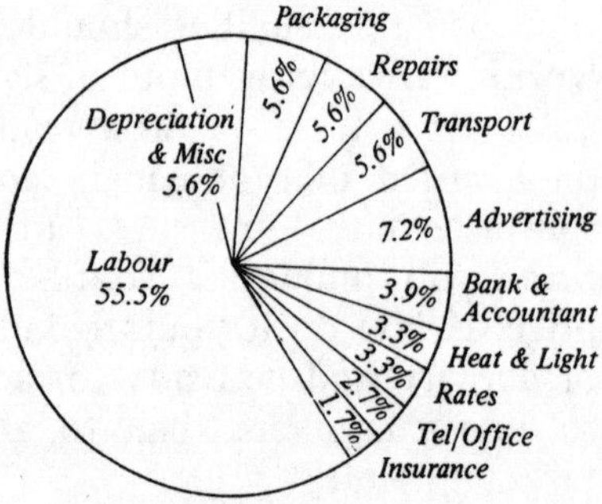

Note: The figures relate to a farm shop with takings of £1000–£2000 per week from the sale of home-grown fruit and vegetables ('sold' from farm to shop at wholesale prices), and bought-in greengroceries and wholefoods.
Sources: Based on data from Mortimer Hill Farm; private communication with other growers and gleanings from the farming press.

Scale of operation

'There is a serious tendency towards capitalism amongst the well-to-do peasants.' Mao Tse-tung.

Grow 50 acres of wheat and you struggle for survival, grow 500 and you make a living, grow 5000—and employ an investment consultant. Whatever the scale of production the basic techniques, marketing and cost structure are fairly similar.

This does *not* apply to retail sales from the farm. The pin-money enterprise, modest farm shop, and rural superstore are not merely in a different league, they are playing a different ball game.

The pin-money enterprise: Traditionally, the pin-money enterprise has been the domain of the farmer's wife. Now, as times become harder in the farming world, farmers are casting acquisitive eyes at their wives' pin-money activities —could a seemingly lucrative sideline be expanded into a major source of income?

Pin-money enterprises are endlessly diverse (e.g. fresh produce, home-cooked produce, crafts, plants, firewood) but they do share some common characteristics:

* High 'opportunity use' of facilities existing on the farm. Opportunity use means making use of land, labour, buildings, feed or other resources which would otherwise be under-used and which need not be included in the accounts as a formal expense. The classic example is the sale of eggs from a few hens housed in an old shed (no building cost), fed largely on kitchen scraps (low feed costs), tended by the family (no appreciable labour costs), with eggs sold to friends (no packaging or retailing costs).

* Low risk, due to small size of enterprise and low capital inputs.

* Low level of interference from officialdom. The stringent rules for a commercial enterprise may not

The two ends of the scale. Backdoor sales (top) and the rural super-store (bottom).

be applied, or applied less ferociously to a very tiny business venture.

* Low level of commitment to the public. There is no need to be at home from 9 to 6 daily in order to sell a few eggs from the back door.
* Low advertising costs.

The farm shop: The term farm shop implies a serious business capable of making a useful contribution to the farm living. 'Farm shop' covers a diversity of size, character and product range but there are some common features:

* Substantial capital commitments are required for:
  Premises—cost of building or adapting premises.
  Fixtures—heating, lighting, security systems.
  Equipment—scales, tills, coolers, freezers, shelving, counters.
  Layout of premises—expenditure on access, parking, landscaping. These can be heavy investments which have little or no resale value should the business be wound up.
* Substantial running costs. The opportunity value of using existing farm facilities decreases with increasing scale of operation. (You can handle the sales of eggs from 5 but not 500 hens from the farm kitchen.)
* Commitment to customers. Once you have advertised your wares and publicised your opening hours the shop must be open and staffed accordingly. You are captive to your customers.
* Complex legal commitments. Operating on a commercial scale involves compliance with many aspects of the law (see under 'Officialdom'). Numerous rules and regulations aim to safeguard health, safety, the environment, and fair play. The rules are intrinsically sensible, but there are a great many of them! Once you open your farm gates to the public you cut across the activities of many different authorities and the hassle involved may seem out of all proportion to the size of your enterprise. If bureaucracy drives you crazy stick to primary production.

The rural superstore: A few farmers have taken the leap from farm shop into the world of Big Business. The farm -situated superstore generally starts with PYO and farm shop, grows, and ultimately expands over several acres and may include a garden centre, leisure activities, refreshments, and other enterprises such as freezer centre, pet food store, camping centre and gift shop. Such ventures are characterised by: enormous capital inputs, separation of retailing and farming activities, a high proportion of bought-in goods and loss of working farm atmosphere. The 'supermarket in a rural setting' generally outgrows its farming origins even though it retains its farm drive and rustic embellishments.

Growth: A pin-money enterprise can make steady growth—up to a point. This point is reached when the venture outgrows the available 'opportunity use' of facilities such as buildings or spare labour. Growth beyond this point—from pin-money enterprise to farm shop, is likely to demand considerable capital inputs for building and equipment and a serious commitment of family labour. It is a leap and should be taken only if you are certain that your enthusiasm and your potential clientele will warrant it.

A farm shop should be planned to accommodate future expansion. If all goes well steady growth will occur until, eventually, the existing facilities such as shop space, parking, management time, are again fully utilised. Growth from farm shop to rural superstore involves another leap, with frightening inputs of capital, and complex management (associated with the probable need to draw in customers from far afield and the likely diversification of product range). This leap is even more hazardous and should not be contemplated without detailed cost/benefit studies. You need to be aware of these patterns of expansion and plan accordingly. *'You cannot cross a chasm in two small jumps.'* – David Lloyd George.

Security

Security is another area of retailing which grows from a minor issue in the small family-run shop to a major consideration in a large retailing business especially if it is remote from the farm dwelling.

Security of buildings: If you stock high-value produce and your farm shop building is not near the farmhouse you will need to take security precautions to reduce the likelihood of theft or vandalism. The police have a crime prevention department which can advise you about security measures.

Security of cash: Try to keep the minimum of cash on the premises. Obviously you must have sufficient change to meet a heavy demand. This is especially important at bank holidays and busy summer weekends when you have the double problem of banks being shut and of people driving out with no small change in their pockets.

Empty the tills frequently on a busy day. Bank the takings frequently. Bank locally and make use of the nightsafe facilities. (The bank provides boxes for the money and you seal these with a coded seal. The sealed boxes can be dropped into the safe at any time of the day or night; this is particularly useful at weekends.)

Pilfering: Pilfering is unlikely to be a problem in the small family-run shop. In a larger operation it is realistic to be aware of the temptations you are offering and to minimise the opportunities for pilfering of goods or cash. Trade journals frequently carry articles on PYO and shop security stressing the need for strict rules and procedures to be used by staff when goods or cash change hands. It is generally considered in the retail trade that 15% of losses are due to short delivery, 25% to theft by customers and 60% by staff (Barletta, 1988).

Security of staff: People are more important than money. Make it clear to everyone working in the shop that if there is the slightest feeling of personal threat—forget the tills: scarper. Think through the retreat routes and means of alerting help. Make sure everyone knows what to do in case of emergency but do not dwell on it. These are simply contingency arrangements and do not need constant reiteration.

Signposts

'I think that I shall never see
A billboard lovely as a tree.
Perhaps, unless the billboard fall
I'll never see a tree at all.' Ogden Nash.

An effective sign enables a customer to locate a farmshop and identify its wares; the less non-essential information the better. It is worth spending time and money on road signs. The image they create can attract or deter regardless of what is actually on the farm. The aim is to combine maximum effectiveness with minimum interference to the landscape—difficult goals to reconcile.

111

The image a sign creates can attract or deter, regardless of what is on the farm.

Legal restraints: The Department of the Environment (DOE) is responsible for the regulations governing what signs you may display and where you may display them. Their criteria concern 'amenity' and 'public safety'. The regulations are set out in *Town and Country Planning (Control of Advertisements) Regulations 1984.* Their administration is in the hands of individual planning authorities, usually the district council of the area in which the sign is to be displayed.

The regulations give 'deemed consent' for certain types of sign. This means that you can go ahead without specific permission from the local authority. The DOE publishes two booklets detailing the types of sign which may benefit from deemed consent. (Copies of the booklets are available on request from the DOE, Tollgate House Annexe, Room TX 308, Houlton St., Bristol, BS2 9DJ.) Deemed consent applies only to a limited range of signs. Definitions are complex. Rough translation from legal jargon suggests that the following might be included:

* A sign giving the name of the farm.
* A sign giving the name of the business.
* Certain types of temporary signs.
* Certain types of signs on business premises.
* Certain types of signs on forecourts of business premises.
* Flags flying from a flagstaff on the roof of the premises.

In all cases there are strict stipulations governing size of sign, number of signs that may be displayed, location of signs in relation to the highway and to buildings. In some areas, designated as 'Areas of Special Consent', the deemed consent is even more restricted. For situations not covered by deemed consent you must apply to the local planning authority for 'express consent'.

The display of signs and advertisements in breach of the 1984 regulations is an offence. Before putting up a sign, take the following steps:

—Do your homework. Read the 1984 Regulations. If you prefer a pre-digested version consult the *NFU Legal Guide* (NFU 1987) pages 25–28.

—If you are a tenant make sure you have the landowner's permission for any sign or advertisement you wish to display.

—Find out from your local planning authority whether you are in an Area of Special Control.

—If you are quite confident that your signs qualify for deemed consent—go ahead.

—If in doubt, or if you need express consent, consult your planning authority.

Should your application for express consent be refused, you may appeal to the Secretary of State for the Environ-

There are strict stipulations governing the size of sign, the number that can be displayed and their location.

ment. The DOE advises '. . . *bearing in mind that these signs are usually displayed in rural areas, an appeal is more likely to be successful if the proposed sign is of reasonable size (i.e. not exceeding say 4 feet x 3 feet), confined to essential information and in a compatible colour scheme (say brown, green, black or white) and sited in such a position that it has a background of a hedge or a tree and does not stand out like a sore thumb'* (DOE, 1986).

Staffing

Take the utmost care over staffing. Friendly, helpful staff contribute greatly to the 'feel' of the shop, making or breaking the atmosphere that stamps a farm shop as uniquely yours.

The small farm shop: Setting up a small farm shop suggests that you or your family are likely, at least initially, to take on the work yourselves. This has several advantages:

*   Minimise initial running costs.
*   Get the feel of the shop and the work involved.
*   Establish personal contact with customers and get feedback from the customers.

The farming adage *'There's no muck like the heel of the farmer'* could well be extrapolated to *'There's no PR like the welcome from the wife'*.

Even for the smallest of shops you will need occasional help at the ready to cover periods of peak sales, holidays and sickness. Without such help you will become a prisoner to the shop and grow to resent it rather than to enjoy it.

Coping with the public is a very different experience from farm work and most farmers will resent being plucked from the fields in order to serve in the shop for a few hours. The best bets for help in the farm shop are likely to be housewives with school-age children (for weekdays during term-time) combined with older children or students at weekends and in the holidays. Part-time helpers generally enjoy the break from home or school and enjoy meeting a variety of people. Women seeking a job to fit in with their family, and students seeking work experience are often of a very high calibre and capable of taking full responsibility. They are usually prepared to be flexible to fit in with the seasonal farm shop needs (providing you respect *their* needs when family or exams take priority).

Employing part-time staff on a casual basis obviates some of the legal obligations and restrictions which beset employers. Nevertheless you must keep a record of staff employed and wages paid. You must have insurance cover for employees while at work (*Employers Liability (Compulsory Insurance) Act 1969* and *Employers Liability (Defective Equipment) Act 1969*).

Staff training on a small scale presents no problem. Work together with your helpers and they will soon fit into your ways.

The larger shop: Even in a larger shop there is much to be said for part-time staff to assist family labour or paid management. Permanent or full-time staff who work more than 16 hours a week and have been employed for more than two years are protected by employment legislation and require contracts or written statements of employment. You will also have to deal with their National Insurance and tax. This is no problem if the farm already employs labour and you can latch into an existing wages system. (If not, apply for details to the nearest Tax Enquiry Office; you can find it under Inland Revenue in your local telephone directory. Be warned though: a fair amount of your precious time saved by having staff in the shop will now be spent on bookwork and form-filling.)

Rates of pay are set down by the Wages Councils (Office of Wages Council, Steele House, 11 Tothill Street, London SW1 H9HF). Send for the relevant leaflets and display them where staff can see them. Wages are age-related. Start youngsters at the minimum rate but be ready to increase this, regardless of age, as soon as they show their worth. It is worth paying well for good work. You are likely to get more work done by one happy, willing lad treated generously than by two lads moaning about minimum wages. You will also have a much happier atmosphere.

Communication: Make sure staff know what is expected of them. Define hours of work and duties. Be firm, but fair and approachable. Provide plenty of opportunities for discussing work and airing grievances (yours and theirs) —avoid the build up of smouldering resentment. Encourage initiative and interest in shop and farm. Talk shop with the staff and welcome their suggestions and comments.

Training

It is fatuous to give detailed advice on training of staff— so much depends on the type of business and particular circumstances. The Agricultural Training Board (ATB) runs occasional courses in Farm Shop Management and related topics. The Retail Fruit Trade Federation runs a training programme for shop assistants (details from the City and Guilds of London Institute or from the Retail Fruit Trade Federation). Look out also for short courses or conferences arranged by the RDC., County Agricultural Colleges; the FSPA and ADAS (addresses given in Appendix 2).

Training in farm shop management is beginning to spread. For instance, Otley College of Agriculture and Horticulture (Ipswich, Suffolk, IP6 9EY) is taking into account the increasing need for farmers and growers to have knowledge of retailing, so their BTEC National Diploma in Business and Finance now includes farm shop studies.

Initially the best form of training for new staff is to work alongside you or a trained member of staff. Let them get the feel of the shop while you work on the till, then change over. You need to sense when to be there, when to retreat to the background, when merely to be on call and when to hand over. It is important to give your staff the experience and confidence of being left in charge. Training (formal or otherwise) must include:

* Public Relations: The importance of a good atmosphere in the shop, talking to customers, dealing with enquiries, suggestions, and complaints.
* Knowledge of products sold and knowledge of the farm.
* Technical skills: Ability to handle scales and tills, working practices and procedure.
* Display, presentation and pricing of goods.
* Health, safety and hygiene.
* Trade legislation.
* Emergency procedures. Everyone in the shop must know what to do in case of fire, illness, accident or personal threat. Make sure a contact is always available in case of emergency.

Uniform

Whether or not you dress yourself and your staff in uniform is a matter of taste and of 'farm shop image'. One school of thought advocates uniforms, badges and name-cards to advertise the business and help give the shop and the staff a sense of identity. This may be valid for the larger shop: it does, however, have the danger of echoing the supermarket.

The opposing school of thought stresses that it is largely the individuality of the staff that creates the 'feel' of the shop. Thus, individual sense of dress (providing it is clean and practical) and of style is part and parcel of the farm shop image.

Take your pick. Both views are valid—they simply apply to very different types of shop. Two general points are:
* Clean overalls are essential if handling 'open' foods such as bulk cheese or unwrapped baked goods.
* T-shirts with logos or some sort of identification are useful at busy times so that customers can identify staff at a glance. This is especially useful for PYO farms with outdoor staff to guide the customers.

Value Added Tax (VAT)

'But in this world nothing can be certain except death and taxes.' Benjamin Franklin, 1789.

Value Added Tax (VAT) is a tax on sales and services. The standard rate of tax is at present 15%; it is imposed on inputs into a business and sales from a business. However, most foods are at present zero-rated which means that no VAT is payable on them.

All businesses with sales over £23,600 (1989) are required to register for VAT. If your farm business is already registered, you will probably be advised to submit joint returns for farm plus shop.

So long as you sell only zero-rated goods (broadly speaking all non-luxury foods including fruit, vegetables, milk, meat and eggs) you will not be required to charge your customers VAT on sales, but you will be able to reclaim VAT paid out on inputs. Thus you will benefit from a VAT refund.

If you retail taxable goods (crafts; toys; pet foods; flowers; luxury foods such as ice cream, chocolates, fruit juices) you will pay 15% VAT on their purchase price, and you must charge your customers 15% VAT on the selling price: in effect, your business acts as a collecting agent for VAT—you hand over to H.M. Customs and Excise the difference between the VAT paid on purchases and collected on sales. As the name implies, the tax that you pay is a tax on the value that you have added by virtue of your trading.

What does VAT entail in practice?

* If your farm business is already registered for VAT simply add shop transactions to the farm transactions when you complete your returns. Remember to include details of any taxable goods sold.

* If your farm was not previously tax-registered but the addition of a farm shop pushes outputs above the £23,600 threshhold you must register for VAT.

* If farm-plus-shop output is less than £23,600 but you consider that your business would suffer if you are not registered (this is likely to happen if you use taxable inputs to produce zero-rated foods) you should consider applying for voluntary registration.

Ask your local VAT offices for advice (you will find them under 'Customs and Excise' in your local telephone directory).

Keeping VAT records is not difficult once you have acquired a routine. Seek advice from the VAT office or from your accountant to get you started. There are various schemes for calculating VAT on retail outputs—you will need to select the scheme best suited to your particular business.

In practice:

—Make sure you get VAT receipts on all your purchases. For each invoice keep a record of gross payment, VAT, and net payment and list these in VAT book or ledger.

—Make sure you charge VAT on all taxable goods sold and keep a record of all such sales.

—Complete your quarterly VAT returns promptly and accurately. Keep details of your calculations to guide you in filling in your next returns and to make life easier for the VAT inspector on his periodic visits. Do seek advice from your local VAT offices if you have any questions. Do not 'muddle through'; work out a routine recording system and stick to it.

Weights and measures

Shop scales and measuring equipment must be accurate. They are liable to periodic inspection by your County Council Weights and Measures Department *(Weights and Measures Act, 1985)*. If you buy second-hand scales check that they have been approved as fit for shop use. Inspectors carry out careful tests on the accuracy of all scales. The scales you use at the check-out have to be highly accurate. A greater level of tolerance is allowed for the spring or balance scales for customers' use in a self-service shop (such scales should be labelled 'for customer use'). The accuracy of scales is in everyone's interest: the periodic checks are reassuring rather than frightening!

The Inspector also checks the accuracy of the weights of prepacked goods and produce labelling. Package weights must be accurate and strict tolerance levels are laid down. In practice you are unlikely to go wrong if you use electronic scales, work carefully and always err on the side of generosity.

Regulations stipulate the way that food may be

sold—loose, prepacked or in special containers. Where pre-packed, the permissible weights are stipulated. For instance, potatoes may be sold unpacked (by net weight) but if pre-packed they must be in units of ½ lb, ¾ lb, 1 lb, 1½ lb or multiples of 1 lb, or else in 500 g, 1 kg, 1½ kg, 2 kg, or multiples of 2½ kg up to and including 25 kg; the weight must be stated on the packaging.

The same applies to processed produce such as jam. If you make a few pots of preserves simply to sell in your own small shop the authorities may deal kindly with you. If you sell processed produce to wholesalers or to other retail shops you will have to comply with a plethora of very strict standards of weight and labelling—failure to comply may cost you dear. Seek guidance from your local Weights and Measures Department (you will find them under 'Trading Standards' in the telephone directory).

Xenophobia

The Oxford English Dictionary defines it as *'morbid dislike of foreigners'*. Farmers who are open to the public recognise it as that morbid 'end-of-season, anti-social, when-will-the-farm-be-ours-again?' sort-of-feeling. It makes a convincing argument in favour of winter closing (see 'Opening times, season'). Take a winter holiday, recharge the batteries and you will be able to give the customers a *genuine* welcome in the spring.

Youth

Children can be endured or enjoyed. Enjoyment is preferable. Make them welcome and give them things to do—play areas, animals to feed, farm trail and quiz, educational exhibits and refreshments. This diverts them away from the shop and keeps them happy. Happy children make for a happy atmosphere: they will bring their parents back for repeat shopping trips. They will, eventually, grow into farm shop customers.

Zest

Zest—you will need it if you are going to enjoy setting up and running a farm shop.
GOOD LUCK!

References

ADAS (1984) *Cash flows in Agriculture*. ADAS SEFM 84/09 (Farm Management Division, Coley Park, Reading, RG1 6DT).

Barker, J. W. (1981) *Agricultural Marketing*. Oxford University Press.

Barletta, M. (1988) *Security in the Shop*. The Grower, March 10th 1988.

Blake, F. (1987) *The Handbook of Organic Husbandry*. Marlborough, Crowood Press. (See Appendix 1)

Davidson, J. H. (1975) *Offensive Marketing*. Pelican Library of Business Management.

DOE (1986) *Notes on Town and Country Planning (Control of Advertisements) Regulations 1984*. Farm Gate Review No. 6 September 1986.

Farm Development Review (1988) *Diversification Update*. 3 (1) 7 1988.

Farmers Weekly (1987) February 6th and 13th 1987.

Farmers Weekly (1988) January 8th 1988. Editorial page 3 and report page 8.

Grower (1988a) *Report of a survey into PYO farms*. April 17th 1988 page 7.

Grower (1988b) Editorial. *User-friendly opportunities*. June 2nd 1988.

Grower Books (1979) *Farm Sales and PYO*. (See Appendix 1).

Honey, C. (1984) *An Investigation into the Establishment and Management of a Farm Shop*. University of Reading. Dissertation for B.Sc. Honours Degree in Agriculture.

Jackson, R. & Nicholson, J. A. H. (1985) *Advertising Pick Your Own*. Farm Business Unit Occasional Paper No. 11. Wye College, University of London.

MAFF (1984) *Direct Farm Sales to the Public*. (See Appendix 1)

MAFF (1987) *New Opportunities in the Countryside. Capital Grants for Farm Diversification*.

MAFF (1988) *New Opportunities in the Countryside. Feasibility Studies and Marketing Grants for Farm Diversification*.

National Food Survey. (Annual) Domestic Food Consumption and Expenditure. MAFF. London: HMSO.

NFU (1987) *Farm Gate Sales to the Public. NFU Legal Guide*. (See Appendix 1)

Nix, J. (1987) *Farm Management Pocket Book*. Wye College, University of London.

Petch, A. (1986) Paper presented at RASE/ADAS Conference *'Adding value to what you produce'*. February 11th 1986.

Slee, B. (1987) *Alternative Farm Enterprises*. (See Appendix 1)

Thompson, P. (1988) Reported in *Farmers Weekly*. January 2nd 1988.

Wendover, W. (1987) Quoted in the *Grower*. December 10th 1987.

PART THREE Appendices

Appendix 1 : Further reading

Blake, F. (1987) *The Handbook of Organic Husbandry*. Marlborough, Crowood Press.
A practical introduction to the practice of organic farming includes a step-by-step guide to conversion from conventional farming to organic production methods for crops and livestock.

British Country Foods Directory. 2nd Edition (1986).
The booklet is published under the joint auspices of the English Tourist Board, Farmers Weekly, Institute of Grocery Distribution, NFU Marketing Division and Royal Agricultural Society of England. It is available from British Country Foods Order Dept., RASE, NAC, Stoneleigh, Warwickshire, CV8 2LZ, at £4.00.
The Directory lists, by product type and by region, more than 400 country-based food products. The booklet is invaluable if you have a farm shop and are looking for suppliers of British produce with a special farming or regional image. It includes both large and small suppliers so it is useful for locating not only the more standard items which your customers can rely on finding in your shop but also the speciality produce to draw in the discerning customer.

Grower Books (1979) *Farm Sales and Pick Your Own*. London: Grower Guide No. 4.
The emphasis in this booklet is on growing and marketing of PYO crops but much of the material (e.g. on advertising) is also relevant to farm shops.
Chapter 7 entitled 'The farm shop—special requirements' deals specifically with the farm shop and the farm supermarket. The section on regulations has been superseded by the *NFU Legal Guide* but the remainder of the booklet, though dated, makes useful background reading for farmgate sales.

Hill, Susan A. (1985) *Specialist Foods*. Institute of Grocery Distribution and NFU.
This study of changes and opportunities in the market for specialist foods makes excellent reading if you are interested in growing the more exotic lines of fruit or vegetables, processing your own produce or buying-in goods for your farm shop.
The author looks at the broad trends in the specialist food market with particular reference to:
*   Fresh produce (such as asparagus, celeriac, artichokes, herbs).
*   Delicatessen type foods.
*   Ethnic foods.
*   Wholefoods.

Lists of wholesale markets, manufacturers and distributors are included. The book is available from the NFU Marketing Division (but costs £40.00 for NFU members or £80.00 to non-members). See if your local library can get it for you; if not try an Agricultural College Library or the NFU Information Centre.

.NFU (1987) *Farm Gate Sales to the Public. NFU Legal Guide.* Shaw and Sons Ltd., Shaway House, London SE26 5AE. Price £3.95 for NFU/FSPA members or £7.95 to non-members.
This booklet is a MUST for anyone contemplating farmgate sales or already running a farm shop. It is a guide to the more important regulations covering the retail sales of farm produce. The introduction states *'It is not intended to be a fully comprehensive guide to the law. If you are in any doubt about how the regulations apply to you, reference should be made to the Statutes and Regulations themselves'* —more than 20 of the more important of these are listed in an Appendix.

Purchase, M. (1987) *Talking Shop. A Guide for the Small Retailer.* EC/Channel 4. Available from the National Extension College, 18 Brooklands Avenue, Cambridge, CB2 2HN at £6.95.
This book *'aims both to encourage and help prospective and in-experienced retailers to tread the right path towards finding, buying, and running their own shop'.* It contains useful advice on the day to day practices involved in running a small shop. The book does not relate specifically to farm shops though the author has experience in running a semi-rural village shop. An easy 'background read' for a farmer with no practical experience of retailing.

Slee, B. (1987) *Alternative Farm Enterprises. A Guide to Alternative Sources of Income for the Farmer.* Ipswich : Farming Press Ltd.
If you are thinking of diversifying, and are still casting around for alternatives, do read this book *before* you go any deeper into farm shops. Bill Slee is senior lecturer in land use at Seale Hayne Agricultural College. His book is an excellent combination of farming perspective, economic and marketing background. The main alternatives are grouped under:
* Tourism and recreation.
* Adding value to conventional products.
* Unconventional agricultural enterprises.
* Use of ancillary buildings and resources.

The Small Firms Service: A useful series of free booklets from the Department of Employment include the following:
* *Starting your own Business—the practical steps*
* *Running your own Business—planning for success*

Appendix 2 : Sources of advice

Diversification into retailing requires different skills from those associated with conventional farming activities. This appendix outlines the advice and support offered by various agencies. The list is not comprehensive but provides a starting point—once within the network it is easy to make further contacts. Other useful sources of information include local library, Chamber of Commerce and Council Offices.

AGRICULTURAL DEVELOPMENT AND ADVISORY SERVICE (ADAS)

Head Office : Ministry of Agriculture, Fisheries and Food, Whitehall, London SW1A 2HH. Tel: 01 233 8226.

There are six regional offices (at Cambridge, Bristol, Leeds, Reading, Trawsgoed and Wolverhampton). Below these are local offices (they are listed in the telephone directory under Agriculture, Fisheries and Food, Ministry of : Agricultural Development and Advisory Services).

Most farmers are familiar with the range of technical services provided by ADAS but perhaps less aware of the availability of management advice and rural enterprise advice (including advice on alternative farm enterprises). Since 1987 ADAS advice is charged for. Initial consultation on farm diversification is free but detailed advice is chargeable.

AGRICULTURAL TRAINING BOARD (ATB)

Address : ATB Training Centre, NAC, Kenilworth, Warwickshire, CV8 2LG.

The ATB arranges a wide range of training courses, including courses on alternative farming enterprises. Also, in conjunction with British Organic Farmers and the Organic Growers' Association, on organic farming.

ASSOCIATION OF INDEPENDENT RETAILERS

Address : Newtown Road, Worcester, WR5 1JX. Tel: 0905 28165.

The aims of the Association are to defend and promote the interests of all independent retailers. Members are given financial support to pursue or defend their legal rights.

THE BRITISH INSTITUTE OF AGRICULTURAL CONSULTANTS (BIAC)

Address : Durleigh House, 3 Elm Close, Campton, Shefford, Beds, SG17 5PE. Tel: 0462 813380.

The BIAC is a professional association of over 200 independent qualified agricultural consultants specialising in various fields including alternative enterprises—few specifically mention Farm Shops as their field of special interest. The Association will supply a list of members on request, or suggest the name of consultants suitable for particular assignments. Members of BIAC are bound by a rigidly enforced code of professional conduct.

COUNCIL FOR SMALL INDUSTRIES IN RURAL AREAS (CoSIRA) see under Rural Development Commission.

ENTERPRISE AGENCIES

Many counties or regions have enterprise agencies which are normally a joint venture between the local authority and the private sector. Their aim is to encourage and promote the growth of the small business sector in their area. The agencies provide free independent counselling and business consultancy, with particular reference to planning, financial control, accounting, marketing, training and premises. Help is offered in the preparation of business plans to put to a bank manager. Some areas administer venture funds to help with capital inputs for selected businesses with growth potential.

Ask at your local library or local authority offices for details of enterprise agencies in your area.

FARM SHOP AND PICK YOUR OWN ASSOCIATION (FSPA)

Address : Agriculture House, Knightsbridge, London SW1X 7NJ.

The Association was started in 1979 with the aim of promoting efficient and professional marketing from the farmgate. It acts as a political pressure group and co-ordinates publicity and advertising. Other activities include conferences, tours and training seminars. It also promotes central purchases of requisites such as packaging materials, signs and recipe leaflets.

HIGHLANDS AND ISLANDS DEVELOPMENT BOARD (HIDB)

Address : 27 Bank Street, Inverness, IV1 1QR. Tel: 0463 234171.

The HIDB offers advice on a wide range of topics. It has a particular interest in non-farming alternatives including tourism, manufacturing and marketing. Advice is free; financial assistance is available on a discretionary basis.

THE MANPOWER SERVICES COMMISSION

For address of your nearest office look in the telephone directory under Manpower Services Commission : Training Division.

Enterprise Allowance Scheme: The scheme is aimed to help the unemployed to start their own businesses. It provides an allowance of £40 per week for up to one year to supplement the income from a new business whilst it becomes established. The scheme is open only to those receiving unemployment or supplementary benefit so is unlikely to apply to a farmer setting up a farm shop. It may however be relevant in the case of an unemployed son or daughter who is interested in starting up a farm shop or a craft venture; the new venture must be entirely independent of the farm business but could perhaps rent redundant buildings from the farm. Details of the scheme are outlined in a booklet available from any Job Centre.

Training: The Manpower Services Commission is funded by the Department of Employment. It runs several training programmes:

* Business Enterprise Programme. A free course for those planning to run, or who have recently set up their own business.

* Private Enterprise Programme. For owners and managers of existing small businesses, this programme consists of 13 one-day training sessions on subjects ranging from sales promotion to taxation. The courses are free if you have been running your business for less than a year, otherwise a small fee is payable.

* Training grants for employers. Local Consultancy grants are available for promoting staff training plans.

NATIONAL FARMERS UNION (NFU) MARKETING DIVISION
Address : 4 St. Mary's Place, Stamford, Lincs, PE9 2DN. Tel: 0780 51513.

Business services, for NFU members only, include business development and administrative advice, market intelligence, legal advice and contact with specialist advisers. The Marketing Division, in association with other agricultural bodies, compiles the *'British Country Foods Directory'*. (See Appendix 1)

The NFU has combined with the Meat and Livestock Commission (MLC) to offer livestock producers specialist advice on selling meat in farm shops. The service provides a free initial consultation with a fee for subsequent detailed advice. The service includes professional advice on cutting methods, display, presentation, labelling, temperature control and hygiene practice. Help can also be given with preparation of business plans, feasibility studies, market research and cost control. For further information telephone the NFU marketing division or the MLC home marketing department at Milton Keynes (0908 648564) or local offices of the MLC.

NATIONAL INSTITUTE OF FRESH PRODUCE
Address : 308 Seven Sisters Road, Finsbury Park, London N4 2BN.

The Institute is sponsored by the Worshipful Company of Fruiterers, the NFU, the National Federation of Fruit and Potato Trades, the Retail Fruit Trade Federation, and the Food, Drink and Tobacco Industry Training Board.

The aim of the Institute is to encourage and promote training for the retail fruit, vegetable and flower trade. Activities comprise courses and training in fresh produce handling. Publications include booklets on fresh fruit retailing and staff training.

ORGANIC ADVISORY SERVICE

Address : c/o Elm Farm Research Centre, Hamstead Marshall, Newbury, Berks, RG15 OHR. Tel: 0488 58298.

An organic farming advisory service, with a team of four consultants, was launched in 1987 as joint development of the Soil Association, Organic Growers' Association and British Organic Farmers. The service is based at the Elm Farm Research Centre near Newbury. It provides on-farm advice; conversion planning; soil analysis. Consultancy fees are charged.

The addresses of the main organic organisations are:

1. British Organic Farmers (Tel: 0272 299666).
2. Organic Growers' Association (Tel: 0272 299800).
3. Soil Association (Tel: 0272 290661).

All above at : 86–88 Colston Street, Bristol, BS1 5BB.

4. Organic Farmers and Growers Ltd., Abacus House, Station Yard, Needham Market, Suffolk, IP6 8AT. Tel: 0449 720838.

RETAIL FRUIT TRADE FEDERATION

Address : 108–110 Market Towers, Nine Elms Lane, London SW8 5NS. Tel: 01 720 9168.

The Association represents the interests of the independent greengrocer. It serves as a political pressure group and provides a range of services including legal guidance, insurance services, information and advice. It publishes the monthly *Retail Fruit Trade Review*.

RURAL DEVELOPMENT COMMISSION (RDC) Formerly CoSIRA.

Address : 141 Castle Street, Salisbury, Wilts, SP1 3TP. Tel: 0722 336255.

The RDC is an agency of the Development Commission which has offices in most of the counties which contain Rural Development Areas. Their aim is to regenerate the rural areas through information and training services. Advice is given on business management (including accounting, marketing and production management); conversion of redundant farm buildings; and technical matters. The RDC has considerable experience and interest in promoting rural shops, and runs excellent courses on setting up and management of small shops—largely relevant also to farm shops. Initial consultation is free. Specialist advice, and courses are charged for.

SCOTTISH AGRICULTURAL COLLEGES, SCOTTISH EXTENSION SERVICES

Address : Cleeve Gardens, Oak Bank Road, Perth, PH1 1HF. Tel: 0738 36611.

Advisory services are equivalent to those of ADAS. Diversification advice is free.

THE SMALL FIRMS SERVICE

(Dial 100 and ask the operator for Freephone Enterprise, or look up the address under Small Firms Centre in the telephone directory.)

This service, sponsored by the Department of Employment, provides information and counselling to help owners and managers of small businesses with their plans and their problems. There is also an advisory service for those starting up a business. The 'counselling service' and the 'business development service' allow for three free sessions, a modest charge is made for further sessions or specialist advice. A useful series of booklets, all free, deals with various aspects of starting and running a business.

TOURIST BOARDS

English Tourist Board, Thames Tower, Hammersmith, London.
Scottish Tourist Board, Ravelston Terrace, Edinburgh.
Welsh Tourist Board, Brunel House, Fitzalan Road, Cardiff.

The tourist boards aim to encourage the provision and improvement of tourist attractions and facilities. Their help may be useful to the farmer who is considering setting up leisure facilities on the farm. Advice is free and some discretionary grants are available. Publications include useful booklets on: Signposting (DG13); How to Start a Small Restaurant or Tea Room (DG16); How to Approach a Bank for Finance (DG18).

Index